The Little Flowers of Saint Francis

the Little Flowers
of SAINT FRANCIS

Brother Ugolino

Introduced, annotated, arranged chronologically,
and rendered into contemporary English by Jon M. Sweeney

PARACLETE HERITAGE EDITION

PARACLETE PRESS
BREWSTER, MASSACHUSETTS

2017 Second Printing Paperback Edition
2016 First Printing Paperback Edition
2011 First Printing Hard Cover Edition

The Little Flowers of Saint Francis

The hard cover edition of this title was cataloged with the Library of Congress as follows:
        Library of Congress Cataloging-in-Publication Data
Fioretti di San Francesco. English.
    The little flowers of Saint Francis / [ascribed to] Brother Ugolino; introduced, annotated, arranged chronologically, and rendered into contemporary English by Jon M. Sweeney.
        p. cm. — (Paraclete heritage edition)
    Includes bibliographical references (p.   ).
    ISBN 978-1-55725-784-0
1. Francis, of Assisi, Saint, 1182–1226 —Legends. I. Ugolino, di Monte Santa Maria. II. Sweeney, Jon M., 1967- III. Title.
    BX4700.F63E5 2011
    271'.302—dc22
                                    2011011005

10 9 8 7 6 5 4 3 2

Published by Paraclete Press
Brewster, Massachusetts
www.paracletepress.com
Printed in the United States of America

CONTENTS

PART II – STORIES OF FRIARS FROM THE PROVINCE OF THE MARCHES

CHAPTERS

INTRODUCTION

ONE OF THE MOST REMARKABLE SPIRITUAL BOOKS ever written, *The Little Flowers of Saint Francis* was originally penned in the mountains of rural Italy by friends of a deceased saint. Since first committed to paper, these stories of St. Francis have been told in order to inspire. For centuries, people have read *The Little Flowers* to become better followers of Jesus.

The book was originally written in Latin—the lingua franca of all serious Christian work in those days—and given the title *Actus Beati Francisci et Sociorum Eius*, which translates as "The Deeds of Blessed Francis and His Companions." From that came a translation into Italian—a budding vernacular in the late thirteenth and early fourteenth centuries—as *Fioretti di Santo Francesco d' Ascesi*, or "The Little Flowers of Saint Francis of Assisi."* Today we usually call it simply *The Little Flowers*.

Many of the stories in *The Little Flowers* are known to us from other biographical sources written at about the same time. In some cases, the stories here are expanded or made more florid; in other cases, stories here appear for the first time.

Amazingly, this collection wasn't translated and published in English until 1864, more than four

---

* These are sometimes called *Actus* and *Fioretti*, for short.

centuries after they were first published in Latin and then Italian. Those first decades after it appeared were a time of flowery Victorian and Edwardian writing, and sentimental rhapsodizing on the beauty of *The Little Flowers* was commonplace in spiritual literature. I have a fondness for this sort of literature because of its earnestness, as when one such writer describes the issue of authorship of these tales with these sentences:

> The *Fioretti*, if you must needs break a butterfly on your dissecting-board, was written, as I judge, by a bare-foot Minorite of forty; compiled, that is, from the wonderings, the pretty adjustments and naïve disquisitions of any such weather-worn brown men as you may see to-day toiling up the Calvary to their Convent.[1]

Similar to the rhapsody just quoted, I've long been convinced that the title of this work stands in the way of its becoming more generally popular today. *The Little Flowers*—the title given to it by the editors of the first Italian edition—reeks with sentiment. It is a title that probably only speaks to the already converted. In English, a metaphorical "flower" still feels somewhat one-dimensional, but *fioretti* could just as easily be translated "blossoms," a word that connotes more of a sense of becoming. It might also help to explain that *fioretti* was also common in early Italian to colloquially connote a collection—somewhat akin to how we might use the adjective "bunch," (another botanical word) today. The negative reaction that the metaphor "little flowers" sometimes inspires made me more than once consider changing the title for the purposes of this new, contemporary English edition of these stories. But that idea was just as quickly discarded; it would be an injustice to so great a classic. Regardless, I recognize how true it is that *The Little Flowers* is perhaps a title that feels irrelevant to many people today who might otherwise benefit from these examples of basic humanity borne in faithfulness to the vision of Christ.

THE QUESTION OF AUTHORSHIP

St. Francis died in 1226, and it was not until a century later—during the 1320s—that these tales were first collected in a serious fashion. Together, the stories represent the singular vision of Francis of Assisi for his time. Brother Leo, Francis's closest friend, was surely one of their early authors, but he was not their final editor. Leo mostly passed them on orally to the other friars who were anxious to preserve the original vision of the early Franciscan movement.

It was an anonymous Italian translator—working during the 1370s—who added some additional stories about St. Francis receiving the stigmata, and these are included in some editions. But for reasons of space as well as an intention to present only the original collection, those stories are excluded here.

The influential seventeenth-century Irish Franciscan scholar Luke Wadding ascribes the original edition of the *Actus* to Friar Ugolino of Monte Santa Maria, whose name occurs three times in the work. Still, most scholars who have studied the text have concluded that it is likely the work of many hands. The first modern biographer of St. Francis, Paul Sabatier, declared the *Fioretti* to be so widely diverse in authorship that it will always remain anonymous. Some of the friars mentioned in the text are probably also among its authors.

About the Book

The Little Flowers tells the story of St. Francis and his earliest companions—the men and women of the early Franciscan movement. They are teaching tales, intended to motivate the reader toward holiness. There is never a question as to the sanctity of the subject of these tales; they are not the subject of objective history. They fit historically into the period of writings about Francis that began with St. Bonaventure's "Major Legend," or "Life of St. Francis" (finished in 1263), telling the details of Francis's life while explaining the many-faceted ways of his unusual sanctity. For example, it was in Bonaventure that we first heard a story, probably of dubious foundation in actual fact, that a simple Assisan man used to lay down his coat in the road for Francis Bernardone to walk on as he passed by, when he was still a young boy. Today's modern reader cannot help sensing some mythmaking in tales such as these, whether they appear in Bonaventure's "Life of Francis," or in *The Little Flowers*. One of the great Franciscan scholars of a century ago, Father Cuthbert, explains this best of all: "Now the writer of the *Fioretti* has no thought of driving anybody; he sets the brethren before us as one who would say, 'Look and see the beauty of their lives and withhold your admiration, if you can!'"[2] (More on this, below.)

The characters in these stories are the closest of friends, working together as comrades, living together as family. The Italian words *frate* and *fratello* are close cousins. Both can mean "brother," although *frate* is a religious brother (or friar) and *fratello* generally indicates a biological brother. The nature of these tales is that the two meanings of *brother* tend to conflate.

There are 53 chapters, most of them quite short. In the earliest manuscripts, the chapters are usually prefaced with a short summary from an editor's hand. I have provided these summaries as well, but only in the form of short chapter titles.

Stories 42–53 are grouped separately from the first 41. This is because while the first 41 are clearly about St. Francis and his earliest companions, the latter group is about friars who were part of the "Spirituals" faction at the time when the *Fioretti* was being composed. These were men of a later generation. The fact that these later stories are presented together with the earlier 41 is part of the slight polemic surrounding the *Fioretti*, as follows: Within a few years of Francis's death, his followers became deeply divided between a smaller group of those who wanted to remain absolutely faithful to the founder's teachings and a larger group of those who viewed his teachings as more temporary. The latter were the leaders of the order. They revered Francis as much as their traditional counterparts, but viewed his role as founder in a different light. Known as the "Conventuals," these leaders believed that Francis's Rule and Testament were important foundational documents but were also open to interpretation by subsequent generations of friars according to needs of a new day. In contrast, the traditionalists or "Spirituals" felt that Francis's teachings were immovable, almost akin to Scripture, in their most conservative moments.

As often happens in such cases, the two sides tended to move to the ideological extreme edges of their positions. The battle was pitted and fierce between the Spirituals, who were probably named derisively, and the Conventuals, who were in authority. In the midst of this, the *Fioretti* was a text produced by the Spirituals, telling stories mostly about friars who were living in friaries in the Marches, the remote part of Italy where they were sometimes quite literally hiding from their brethren, and was intended to aid their cause.

There are other differences between the tales in part 1 and those in part 2. For instance, in contrast to the brief episodes of part 1, part 2 focuses on lengthy profiles of specific friars—almost mini-Lives of them. And then, theologically, there are some small differences. For example, in part 2 there is a preoccupation with the late medieval doctrine of purgatory (a place where souls must be purified before possibly going on to heaven), which was not made formal in the Roman Catholic Church until 1274 at the Second Council of Lyon, nearly a half century after St. Francis's death.

THE CHRONOLOGICAL PROBLEM

The Little Flowers never claims to be a work of history. For example, we meet St. Clare in the fifteenth story, after she has already become a sister, and we are never treated to the dramatic story of Clare's first coming to join St. Francis and the early friars—traditionally assigned to March 20, 1212. That comes from other sources. Instead, the first time we meet Clare is when she comes to eat a meal with Francis and his brothers at St. Mary of the Angels in the valley below Assisi. Similarly, in the second story—the one about Brother Bernard's becoming the first follower of Francis—we hear reference to Francis using stones to build churches, and we are introduced to the term *Friar Minor*, both of these things without any additional information or context. A reader has to turn to the early biographies of Francis for these things. Similarly, the stories in this book do not follow a narrative of any kind. In this respect, they bear all of the marks of a compiled work. Had they been written by one author, that author would surely have striven to link them together more clearly and chronologically.

I believe that today's reader is sometimes prevented from the full benefit of *The Little Flowers* by what I call their chronological problem. They simply don't fit a narrative as they have been traditionally arranged. Today's readers would benefit from having these tales put into an approximate order of their happening.

For example, in the traditional order, the transition from chapter 2 to chapter 3 can be alarming. Chapter 2 is the story of Brother Bernard's conversion, while Francis was still very young in his own religious life; but suddenly, chapter 3 begins with: "The devout servant of Christ crucified, Francis, had lost his sight. Nearly blind from all of his severe penances and tears. . . ." This tale is told, not from the 1209 of chapter 2, but from a time at least a decade later. In the present edition, this has become chapter 25. Similarly, chapter 20 in the original ordering is a story of Francis appearing from heavenly glory (after his death) to a young friar; but after this tale come many others where Francis is still alive. All of this is understandably confusing.

This edition of *The Little Flowers* is different. I have arranged the stories in what seems to be the most likely chronological ordering according to what we know of the life of St. Francis and the lives of his early followers. (Some of the stories take place, in fact, *after* Francis's death.) In addition to including at the end of each story, in brackets—like these: [ ]—the traditional numbering of that story in every other edition of *The Little Flowers*, I have also added in brackets at the beginning of the stories the approximate or traditionally understood date or dates for the events taking place.

Each of the tales is dated according to the general consensus of scholars. My sources are listed at the back of the book in a section entitled "For Further Reading." Most often these dates are approximate; occasionally they are precise; and sometimes they are a combination of both. For example, in the thirty-fourth story, "How St. Francis knew that Brother Elias would leave the Order," we can only approximate the beginning, but then we know precisely the end, since it is the occasion of Brother Elias's deathbed conversion (April 22, 1253).

Controversies behind the Surface of These Stories

Are they true? In many places, one has the feeling in these stories of reading legends more than facts. Some people refer to them in words similar to those of Professor Rosalind Brooke of Cambridge University, who calls them a "remarkable work of historical fiction."[3] Another recent scholar calls them "typically metaphorical, mythological."[4] It is true that much of what is in here does not appear in other historical sources. However, others take a more sanguine view, as for instance when Raphael Brown offers an explanation for why so much of what is in *The Little Flowers* doesn't appear elsewhere in the historical record:

> How then can we explain the puzzling fact that many of its most interesting stories were not recorded in the first official biographies of the Saint, which were based on the testimony of a number of his companions, including Leo, Angelo, and Rufino? The answer is quite simple. It is really a matter of psychology. The Poverello's best friends would naturally hesitate to mention—and an official biographer would hesitate to describe—a recently canonized Saint of the Church shaking hands with a wolf or eating nothing for forty days or telling his companion to twirl around in a public crossroad or go into a church and preach a sermon while wearing only his breeches.[5]

Still other scholars value these later tellings of early Franciscan events due to the same fact that it was the friends closest to Francis who are doing the telling. What is perceived weakness for some is strength in the opinion of others. One such scholar is Michael F. Cusato: "Even though a very late source, [the *Fioretti*] bears the traces of a long and cherished oral tradition among the friars who were present with [Francis] on La Verna [for the most important moment of his life, the receiving of the stigmata]."[6]

There's no question that these stories are the result of more than a century of brewing in the hearts and spirits of the early Franciscan movement. For that reason they are simultaneously mistrusted as historical fact and venerated for their ability to communicate something at least as important. Nevertheless, for the casual observer or reader, or the one drawn to spiritual literature for its more literary values, this little book is often the only introduction they receive as to who St. Francis was. For the past 150 years, scholars and readers of all kinds have looked to these stories for hints as to Francis's personality, as much as for confirmation of some of the actual happenings of his eventful life. On this subject Hilaire Belloc once wrote this:

> If there is one thing that people . . . have gone wrong upon more than another in the intellectual things of life, it is the conception of a Personality. . . . The hundred-and-one errors which this main error leads to include a bad error on the nature of history. Your modern non-Catholic or anti-Catholic historian is always misunderstanding, underestimating, or muddling the role played in the affairs of men by great and individual Personalities. That is why he is so lamentably weak upon the function of legend; that is why he makes a fetish of

documentary evidence and has no grip upon the value of tradition. For traditions spring from some personality invariably, and the function of legend, whether it be a rigidly true legend or one tinged with make-believe, is to interpret Personality. Legends have vitality and continue, because in their origin they so exactly serve to explain or illustrate some personal character in a man which no cold statement could give.[7]

There is no document or collection of documents that has had as much impact on our collective and cultural understanding of Francis of Assisi and the personality of the early Franciscan movement as *The Little Flowers*.[8]

As an example of this, the stories here, unlike those in the first biographies of St. Francis written by Thomas of Celano, often take on a deliberate pedagogy. For example, "Three murderous robbers become Franciscan friars" (chapter 29) has the structure in its second half of an analogical journey that was never intended to be factual, but rather a teaching tale. Does that make it any less valuable as evidence of what Francis and his early companions were like? I don't think so.

What makes these stories relevant today is the power with which they grab hold of the reader, sometimes by the fantastic claims they make for the life of St. Francis and his first followers, to change one's life before God. Hyperbole—if that's what it's called—has always been a rhetorical device and a symptom of deep belief; and it can be a tool of transformation. It all reminds me of the story from the tradition of the Desert Fathers and Mothers of the young monk who says in frustration to the elder monk, "What more can I do? I've done all of the spiritual practices. I've said all of the prayers!" And the elder monk holds out his arms, fingers spread dramatically, and replies, "You can become all flame!" Tradition has it that the elder's fingers appeared to be bursting with fire at that moment.

A further word needs to be said about the controversies brewing in the late thirteenth and then fourteenth centuries between the "Spirituals" and the "Conventuals"— those two groups within the Franciscan Order that were in great tension at the time the *Fioretti* was first written down. The serious rift between these two factions comes through clearly in chapter 33, for example, which reads like a polemic for the Spirituals' cause. And then nowhere in this book is the tension more clear than in the story from part 2, "When God showed Brother James of Massa true secrets" (chapter 48). The vision recounted there is one that graphically depicts the tension between the Spirituals, represented by minister-general Brother John of Parma (1247–57), and the Conventuals, represented by Brother Bonaventure, who replaced Brother John in the role of minister-general of the Order. *The Little Flowers* represents the Spirituals' perspective on the life of St. Francis, and when we encounter the themes of evangelical poverty, faithfulness to the original Rule of Francis, the bad character of Brother Elias, and Francis's likeness to Christ, we are receiving a particular perspective. The Spirituals so identified their founder with Jesus Christ that they were thought to have gone to heretical extremes by others. When in the story "St. Francis keeps Lent on an island in Perugia" (chapter 17) the anonymous Spirituals authors write, "It is believed that Francis only ate the half in reverence to the fasting of our Lord, who for forty days and forty nights took nothing at all; so Francis took half a loaf in order to avoid the sin of pride, that he might not follow too closely the example of Jesus Christ," they are comparing their revered founder to Jesus in ways that understandably made more mainstream Franciscans (as well as a few popes) uncomfortable.

Another theme bubbling beneath the surface of these stories is the demonizing of Brother Elias—the second appointed minister-general of the Friars Minor (in 1221). Elias was an early companion of St. Francis and traveled often with him, and became Francis's vicar before the saint's death. However, after Francis's death Elias ruled the order in controversial ways, marginalizing some of Francis's closest friends (the Spirituals), supervising the building of the inappropriately ornate Basilica of San Francesco in Assisi, and then aligning himself with Emperor Frederick II, an action that led to his excommunication. For these reasons, we see a reinterpretation of Elias's earlier days with his close friend Francis in many of the stories in *The Little Flowers*. Elias becomes almost a devil lurking, waiting to pounce, even though other sources tell us that Francis and Elias were the closest of friends for most of their time together.

Above all, the most persistent theme of the Spirituals was the importance of absolute poverty on the part of a true follower of St. Francis of Assisi. Soon after Francis's death, many of his followers began to interpret the call to poverty to mean something other than, or "less than" owning literally nothing, storing nothing, preparing not at all for what might be needed tomorrow. In this way, the Spirituals felt that they were being faithful not only to Francis but to the teachings of Jesus in the Gospels. One can see the authors of these tales pounding away on that theme, for example, in the agenda-filled tale "St. Francis interprets a vision of Brother Leo" (chapter 33).

OTHER THEMES

St. Francis's love for poverty comes through loud and clear in *The Little Flowers*. Slightly beneath the surface in this love is his hand-in-hand championing of local workers, his desire to dispose of extraneous "things," a life of full simplicity, and the rights of ordinary people versus the powerful. He was remarkably ahead of his time in these respects. See "St. Francis praises holy poverty, and lifts Brother Masseo into the air" (chapter 6) for an example of some of this.

There are also moments in these stories where the reader might be surprised by the language used by St. Francis and his friars. Francis was an earthy man just as he was a man of great holiness. He was frank and forthright. And occasionally he was even cEross. In "Brother Rufino is severely tempted by the devil" (chapter 9), you'll see that he was just "common" enough to use one scatological word to forcefully get his very important point across!

In addition to occasional earthly language, there are also sometimes frank discussions of sin and temptation that are unique in late medieval religious literature. For instance, the presence of sexual temptation—even what we today would call sex addiction—is unmistakable in the long tale "The remarkable life of young Brother Simon" (chapter 15). One of the features of the early Franciscans—and surely one of the reasons for the enduring qualities of this classic work—was the way they refused to sugarcoat the troubles that face anyone attempting to live an authentic Christian life.

Another theme that comes through in *The Little Flowers* is St. Francis's unique relationship to religious authority. Many scholars believe that this is a side effect of the Spirituals who compiled and edited the stories rather than an accurate and factual telling of how it truly was. For whatever reason, Francis often seems to "go out on his own" religiously in these stories. Again, see "St. Francis praises holy poverty, and lifts Brother Masseo into the air" (chapter 6) for an example.

A few of the tales are almost genres unto themselves. The most obvious examples of this are "The remarkable life of young Brother Simon" (chapter 15) and "The holy life of Brother John of Penna" (chapter 46), both of which read like short hagiographies, or Lives, of saints. These two narratives match closely the otherworldly, more fantastic, hagiographical style and substance of those saint stories that were collected in Jacobus of Voragine's famous book, *The Golden Legend*. Jacobus did his work in the century before Brother Ugolino pulled together the first Italian edition of *The Little Flowers*. After the Bible and perhaps the *Imitation of Christ*, *The Golden Legend* was the most-read book of the late Middle Ages.

ABOUT THIS EDITION

The 53 tales of this edition of *The Little Flowers* form the traditional core text of the work found in any complete edition. Following the 53 stories are brief biographical sketches of the friars and other notables mentioned in the tales.

In these contemporary English renderings, I have been faithful to the spirit of the stories, and I have compared translations among several excellent editions from the last century. I have attempted on rare occasions to remove the occasional repetition in the original stories. In a few instances I have condensed a paragraph into a sentence or two, but only when it would result in no loss of content, context, or meaning.

―――――――――

1 Maurice Hewlett, *Earthwork Out of Tuscany—Being Impressions and Translations of Maurice Hewlett with Illustrations by James Kerr Lawson* (New York: Macmillan Company, 1902), 38.

2 Father Cuthbert, OSFC, "The Teaching of the *Fioretti*," *The Catholic World*, 89 (1909): 190.

3 Rosalind B. Brooke, *The Image of St. Francis: Responses to Sainthood in the Thirteenth Century* (New York: Cambridge University Press, 2006), 246.

4 Alessandro Vettori, *Poets of Divine Love: Franciscan Mystical Poetry of the Thirteenth Century* (New York: Fordham University Press, 2004), 49.

5 Raphael Brown, ed., *The Little Flowers of St. Francis: First Complete Edition* (New York: Image Books, 1958), 27–8.

6 Michael F. Cusato, *The Early Franciscan Movement (1205– 1239): History, Sources, and Hermeneutics* (Spoleto, Italy: Fondazione Centro Italiano di Studi Sull'alto Medioevo, 2009), 212.

7 Hilaire Belloc, *Selected Essays*, ed. J. B. Morton (Baltimore: Penguin Books, 1958), 141.

8 For this reason I find it astonishing that neither the *Fioretti* nor its author merit an entry in the 1,290-page, two-volume reference work *Medieval Italy: An Encyclopedia*, ed. Christopher Kleinhenz (New York: Routledge, 2004).

PART I
STORIES OF ST. FRANCIS OF ASSISI
AND HIS EARLY COMPANIONS

CHAPTER I

How St. Francis came to have twelve companions

[F E B R U A R Y   2 4 ,   1 2 0 9]

THE FIRST THING YOU MUST KNOW IS THAT ST. FRANCIS was beautifully conformed to Christ in all of the acts of his life. Just as Jesus began preaching and chose twelve disciples to turn away from the world and follow him in poverty and virtue, so too did Francis have twelve companions who followed him when he began to found his Order.

Just as one of Christ's disciples would be a disappointment to God and eventually hanged himself by the neck, so did Francis have a companion such as this, Brother John of Capella, who left the Order and, in the end, hanged himself. To the chosen this remains a lesson for the need of humility and fear. For none can be certain of their own righteousness or their ability to persevere to the end.

Just as the apostles of Christ were renowned for their holiness and example, filled with the Holy Spirit, so too were the first companions of Francis. From the original apostles until now, we have not seen such holy and humble men. One of them, Brother Giles, would be raptured like St. Paul up to the third heaven.[*] Another, Brother Philip, would be touched on the lips by an angel with a coal of fire, just as the Prophet Isaiah once was.[†] Another, Brother Sylvester, spoke with God like a friend, as Moses himself had done. Yet another, by the pure clarity of his mind, soared like an eagle to the light of divine wisdom, just like John the Evangelist. That was Brother Bernard, the most humble of men and yet the most profound of explicators of the meaning of Holy Scripture. And yet one more—Brother Rufino, nobleman of Assisi—was canonized in heaven while he still lived in this world. In these ways, the first companions were each marked with a singular holiness. About these marks, there is much more to tell.

[#1 of 53]

---

[*] "The third heaven" is an uncommon term, but is an allusion to 2 Corinthians 12:2–4 where Paul speaks of himself and his experience on the road to Damascus: "I know a person in Christ who fourteen years ago was caught up to the third heaven—whether in the body or out of the body I do not know; God knows. And I know that such a person . . . was caught up into Paradise and heard things that are not to be told, that no mortal is permitted to repeat" (cf. Acts 9:1–9, 22:6–11). The "first" heaven was the atmosphere of earth; the "second" heaven was where the sun, moon, and stars do their work; and the "third" was regarded as the abode of God.

[†] "Then one of the seraphs flew to me, holding a live coal that had been taken from the altar with a pair of tongs. The seraph touched my mouth with it and said, 'Now that this has touched your lips, your guilt has departed and your sin is blotted out'" (Isa. 6:6–7).

CHAPTER 2

———

The conversion of the first, Brother Bernard

[ca. APRIL 1, 1209–APRIL 16, 1209]

THE FIRST COMPANION TO JOIN ST. FRANCIS WAS Brother Bernard of Assisi. His conversion happened like this.

It was in the days when Francis was still wearing his secular clothing, even though he had begun to renounce the things of the world. He had been going around Assisi looking mortified and unkempt, wearing his penance in his appearance in such a way that people thought he had become a fool. He was mocked and laughed at, and pelted with stones and mud by both those who knew him and those who did not. But Francis endured these things with patience and joy, as if he did not hear the taunts at all and had no means of responding to them.

The noble Bernard of Assisi noticed all of this. For two years, he watched Francis as he was scorned by the townspeople—the same people who respected Bernard as one of the wisest and wealthiest men around. Despite the torment, Francis always seemed patient and serene. Bernard pondered these things in his heart. He said to himself, *This man must have grace that comes from God alone.*

But Bernard decided to put the younger man's saintliness to a test. He asked Francis to join him one night for dinner, and they ate together at Bernard's table.

Then, Bernard invited Francis simply to spend the night; he had prepared a room for Francis in his home, in fact, in his very own chamber. This was a part of the test as well.

In that room a lamp burned low all night long. Francis entered the chamber first, and quickly flung himself into bed, pretending that he was eager to drop off to sleep. Then, Bernard came into the chamber prepared for bed, and he too lay down. Before long, Bernard was pretending to be asleep, even going so far as to let out loud sounds of snoring. Hearing such noises coming from the other end of the chamber, Francis got out of his bed and threw himself to the floor to pray.

Francis turned his face toward heaven and raised his hands fervently to God. "My God, my God!" he cried out.

He began to weep, and he prayed in this way all night long until the morning light.

Why did Francis pray these words, "My God, my God!"? Like a prophet, he could see the great things that God would accomplish through him and through the movement that he would begin—and Francis was considering his inadequacy to do what needed to be done. This was his call to God for help.

Bernard of Assisi saw all of this from the other end of the chamber. The words and spirit of Francis touched him deeply, and in that moment, Bernard felt inspired to change his own life also. By the light of morning, Bernard said, "Friar Francis, I have decided to follow you in your work, to live with you your life, and to leave behind the things of this world."

Francis was elated. He said, "Lord Bernard, what you propose doing is of such importance, and will be so difficult, that I think we should seek together from our Lord Christ how we are to do it. Let's go together to the house of the bishop and hear Mass, and remain in prayer until the time of Tierce, asking God to show us his will three times in the reading of the missal."* And so they went together to the bishop's house and they heard Mass, and they stayed at prayer until the hour of Tierce, and then they asked the priest to take up the missal three times for them.

The priest made the sign of the cross over the book, and opening it the first time he read, "If you wish to be perfect, go, sell your possessions, and give the money to the poor, and you will have treasure in heaven; then come, follow me" (Matt. 19:21). Then the priest opened the book for a second time. There occurred these words: "Take nothing for your journey, no staff, nor bag, nor bread, nor money" (Lk. 9:3). And last, the third opening of

---

* Tierce is one of the appointed canonical "hours" of monastic daily prayer, usually at 9 AM. A missal was the book a priest used for celebrating the Mass. In the thirteenth century, this would have included much of the text of the New Testament (what is now usually included in a separate book called a Lectionary).

the book revealed: "If any want to become my followers, let them deny themselves and take up their cross and follow me" (Mk. 8:34).

When they had heard all of these words, Francis said to Bernard, "This is the wisdom that Jesus Christ has given to us. You should go and do exactly what you have heard. And thanks to God for showing us the true way of life!"

Bernard left immediately to gather all of his possessions. He owned many things, and some he distributed to the poor. Some he sold. And with the money that he earned, he gave liberally to widows and orphans, prisoners and pilgrims. In all of this, Francis was by his side.

While they were distributing money to the poor in Assisi, a man named Sylvester saw and said to Francis: "You never paid me for all of those stones that I gave you to repair churches." Francis was amazed at the man's greed at such a moment as this. He thrust his hand into Bernard's pocket, which was filled with money, and then thrust a handful of money into Sylvester's pocket, saying, "If you ask for more, I will give that, too." Sylvester turned and went home.

Later than evening, Sylvester thought about what he had done, and reproached himself. For three nights, then, he had a dream from God. He saw a cross of gold coming from the mouth of Francis; its arms reached from east to west, and the top of the cross went all the way to heaven. Sylvester knew that the Lord was touching him, and for God's glory he too gave away all that he had to the poor and became a Friar Minor. In some of the stories to come, you will see how Sylvester became a holy man and spoke as an intimate friend with God.

In the same way, Bernard received much grace from God once he'd given everything away. He became a friar with the gift of contemplation. Francis used to say that Brother Bernard should be held in reverence by the others because he was the first to live according to the poverty of the Gospel, holding back nothing, offering himself naked into the arms of the Crucified, glory be to him forever and ever. Amen.

[#2 of 53]

CHAPTER 3

Brother Masseo tests St. Francis's humility

[c a .   1 2 1 0 – 1 2 1 5]

S T. FRANCIS WAS LIVING AT THE PORTIUNCULA[*]
with Brother Masseo of Marignano, a man of holiness
and discernment with many graceful ways of speaking about
divine things, for which Francis adored him much. One day,
Francis was coming back from the woods where he'd been
praying, when Brother Masseo met him alone on the path.
Masseo had gone to find Francis and to test his humility. He
said to Francis, partly in jest, "Why you? Why you?"

"What do you mean, Brother Masseo?" St. Francis
replied.

"I mean, why does the world all seem to run after you,
to want you, to listen to and obey you? You aren't good-
looking. You don't know very much. You aren't of noble
birth. So . . . why *you*?"

Francis heard all of this and felt joy in his heart. He
raised his face toward heaven, feeling caught up in the

---

[*] This was St. Francis's most beloved place in the valley of Spoleto below
Assisi. The structure of the Portiuncula—which was known at that time
by its religious name, *Santa Maria degli Angeli* (St. Mary of the Angels)—was
built in the early Middle Ages, and there is a legend that it was originally
intended to surround relics of the Virgin brought to Umbria from the
Holy Land. The chapel was owned by the Benedictine monks of Monte
Subasio. In 1211, the abbot gave Francis permanent use of it, and Francis
gathered the friars together in small and temporary dwellings around it.

spirit of God. He then came back to the present moment, bowed, and gave praise to God. In a spirited way he turned back to Brother Masseo and said, "You want to know 'why me'? Do you really want to know? I have seen this by the holy eyes of God.

"Those holy eyes have never seen a sinner viler than I am. He chose me, the worst of them all, for he says that he chooses the fools of the world to shame the wise, the low things to reduce the noble and great to nothing—all so that great virtue will be accredited to God alone and never to one of God's creatures."

At this, Brother Masseo was moved and humbled by St. Francis's most humble response. To the glory of God in Christ. Amen.

[#10 of 53]

CHAPTER 4

———

How St. Francis made Brother Masseo turn around and around

[ca. 1210 – 1215]

St. Francis was traveling in Tuscany with Brother Masseo, one of his favorite traveling companions. Brother Masseo knew how to talk with the saint, showed great discretion, and helped Francis to duck the eyes and ears of others when he desired to do so.

On this day, as they were walking on the road together, Masseo a little bit ahead of Francis, they came to a crossroads. It was a spot where they could go to Siena, Florence, or Arezzo. Brother Masseo said, "Father, what road should we take?"

Francis replied, "The road that God desires us to take."

"How will we know that?" Masseo asked.

"By a sign that I will show you. Now, spin yourself around right here and now, twirling in a circle like children who play, and don't stop until I tell you to stop."

Masseo did this, as he was told. He kept turning around in circles until he fell down over and over again, as usually happens when one twirls and gets dizzy in the head. Each time that he stumbled, he got back up and twirled again, not thinking to stop until Francis told him to stop.

After a while, Francis finally said, "Okay, stop!"

Masseo stopped.

Francis asked him, "Now, in which direction do you face?"

"Siena."

"That is the road God wants us to take."

So they traveled on the road to Siena, and Brother Masseo thought about how St. Francis had made him do such a childish thing, and in front of so many other passersby! As they came close to Siena, the people there heard that Francis was coming, and they came out to the road to meet them. They gathered so closely around them that it seemed that the feet of Francis and Masseo hardly touched the ground.

There was a fight going on in Siena at this time, and two people had just been killed. So Francis first went to that place, stood there, and preached to the fighting men. He spoke so beautifully and with such holiness that their fighting ceased. When the bishop heard of this, he invited Francis to his house, welcoming him to stay the night there. But in the morning, Francis and Masseo woke early and left the bishop's house before daybreak.

Brother Masseo wasn't happy about this. He felt that Francis had acted wrongly. He muttered under his breath, "What has the saint done? First he makes me twirl around like a girl, and today he dishonors the bishop?" But then Masseo came to his senses, and felt sorry for his thoughts. He thought to himself, *Brother, you are too proud, passing judgment on what you don't understand. What happened yesterday was clearly God's will.*

Now all of these things going on in Masseo's heart were revealed to Francis by the Holy Spirit. He came up beside Masseo and said, "Hold fast to those thoughts you are having now, for they are the ones inspired by God." Masseo was astounded by this. He could see that Francis knew the secrets of his heart and that divine grace and wisdom surrounded all that he did.

[#11 of 53]

—

CHAPTER 5

St. Francis tests Brother Masseo's humility

[c a . 1 2 1 0 – 1 2 1 5]

S T. FRANCIS WANTED TO HUMBLE BROTHER MASSEO, since Masseo's gifts were so great that he might otherwise get carried away with himself. So one day, while living with those saintly men who were his first companions (including Brother Masseo), Francis said to Masseo before all: "Brother, all of these companions of yours have the gift of contemplation, but you have the gift of preaching. In order that your brothers may have more time and space for prayer and contemplation, I would like you to care for opening the gate to our visitors, giving alms to those who ask for them, and cooking all of our meals. And when we are eating, you are to go outside to eat so that you can be among our visitors and share with them some spiritual words."

Brother Masseo bowed his head and humbly accepted this order from St. Francis. And for the next several days, Masseo was the gatekeeper, the almsgiver, and cook, while his companions spent their time in prayer and contemplation.

After a while, the companions began to feel bad for Masseo, knowing that he was gifted with contemplation probably more so than any of them, and they agreed to ask Francis to redistribute the various duties among them all. Francis heard them, and he agreed. He called Brother Masseo and said to him, "Brother, your companions want to share in the duties that I gave to you."

"Whatever you ask of me, I will do as if I do it for God," Masseo replied.

At this, Francis saw clearly Masseo's humility, and the love of the other companions, and he preached for them a beautiful sermon on these subjects, saying the more graces and gifts that we are given by God, the more that is expected of us.

[#12 of 53]

CHAPTER 6

———

St. Francis praises holy poverty, and lifts Brother Masseo into the air

[c a . 1 2 1 0 – 1 2 1 5]

ST. FRANCIS WANTED TO BE LIKE JESUS IN ALL things, and this even included the way in which he sent his companions out into the world; so he sent them two-by-two. And in order to show them by example, Francis himself went first, and took with him to France, Brother Masseo.

One day as they came to a village and were feeling hungry, for the love of God they went begging for food, according to the teaching of the Rule. Francis took one road through the village, and Masseo, the other. Since Francis was small and insignificant in appearance, he was considered a pauper by all who saw him. Fools see only what's on the outside, and Francis received almost nothing for his effort. But Masseo, since he was tall and handsome, received plenty.

When they finished begging, they came back together to eat just outside of town. With effort, they found a spring that had a bread stone beside it, and on the stone they placed the food that they received. Right away, Francis saw that there was more bread from Masseo's begging, and the pieces were larger too. He was filled at the sight with joy because of his love for poverty. Francis said: "Brother, we don't deserve these great treasures!" He repeated this several times.

"Father, how can this be a *treasure*?" Masseo asked.

"This is exactly what I consider a treasure," Francis replied. "Nothing we have here required the work of others. Everything here has been provided for us by God. I think we should ask God to help our hearts to see the treasures of this—examples of holy poverty at work."

After this, they got up and continued along, singing, on their way to France.

They came to a church, at which Francis said to Masseo, "Let's go inside and hear Mass and pray." But when they went inside, they saw that the priest was not there, and so Francis immediately went behind the altar to pray. While there, he received a vision from God that set his soul on fire. It was as if love flames were coming out of his eyes and mouth. Francis approached Masseo in this state and cried out, "Brother, give yourself to me!" He said it three times, and by the third time Masseo ran to Francis and hugged him. Then Francis was saying, "Ahhhhhh," in the power of the Spirit, and with this holy breath he lifted Masseo up into the air. Masseo was stunned. He later told the companions that it was the most consoled and loved that he ever felt in his life.

After this, the two began to travel toward Rome, because Francis said, "Let us go to St. Peter and St. Paul and ask them to show us how to possess even more the treasures of holy poverty." Then he added, "Poverty is a heavenly virtue, and by it, everything of the earth loses its value. By poverty, a soul may unite with God. Poverty makes the soul, even while earthbound, talk with angels."

In Rome, while talking about such things, they walked into St. Peter's Basilica. Francis and Masseo each went to a corner of the church to pray to God and the holy apostles for the possession of poverty and its treasures. While Francis was in prayer and in tears, the holy apostles appeared before him. They kissed and hugged him and they said, "Brother, because you have requested and desired to do as Christ himself did, and as we the apostles did, our Lord has sent us to tell you that your prayers have been answered. You and your followers will be given the blessings of true poverty." After this, St. Peter and St. Paul disappeared.

Francis rose and went to find Masseo. He asked him if he had received any special revelations in the church. "No," Masseo replied. And then Francis told him of what had happened to him. They were filled with joy and, as it happened, forgot completely about needing to go to France.

[#13 of 53]

CHAPTER 7

———

Christ appears among them

[ca. 1210 – 1215]

ST. FRANCIS DROVE ALL OF HIS THOUGHTS TOWARD Christ, and directed all of his desires to be like Jesus, in all things. On one early occasion, when he was together with his companions, who were still only a few, he began talking about God with his blessed spiritual sons. With fervor, he asked one of them to quickly open his mouth and say something—whatever the Holy Spirit gave to him—to say at that moment. The friar did so, saying something marvelous by the Holy Spirit. Then Francis asked him to be quiet.

Francis then asked another brother to speak similarly. He did, and then Francis asked for his silence.

He then asked a third friar to speak without premeditation, to say something about Our Lord. Like the first two, it was clear that this one spoke with the power of the Holy Spirit. Francis and everyone else there knew so.

One after another that evening, the friars spoke of God and spread beautiful sounds of God's grace all around. Our Lord even appeared among them as a young man. He gave them his blessing—which filled Francis and all of the others with such sweet feelings of holiness that they fainted on the spot. Later, when they came to, Francis said to the gathering: "Brothers, give thanks to Our Lord, who has decided to give some wisdom into the mouths of little children. It is God who opens our mouths and makes our dumb tongues sing."

[#14 of 53]

———

CHAPTER 8

St. Francis cares for a man with leprosy

[c a .   1 2 1 0 – 1 2 1 5]

WHILE HE WAS LIVING IN THIS WORLD, ST. FRANCIS always tried to follow in the footsteps of Jesus, doing as the master had done. As Christ became a man and a pilgrim, so Francis became a pilgrim, even writing in his Rule how all of his followers are pilgrims and strangers in this world.

More important, as Christ was a servant to those who were sick, unclean, and lepers, wishing even to die for them, so Francis, who longed to be like Christ, served those afflicted with leprosy, bringing them food, washing their sores, cleaning their clothes, and even giving them passionate kisses. On many occasions, God healed the soul of such a one, just as Francis healed his body. And so it was that Francis willingly went to those with leprosy, and ordered his friars to do likewise.

It happened on one such occasion that the friars were caring for lepers and other people with illnesses in a hospital. There was a certain man there who was seriously ill and also extremely disagreeable—so much so that people began to wonder if he might be possessed. Not only did this man verbally attack the friars who tried to help him, but he would also strike and hurt them in various ways. Worst of all, he would blaspheme Jesus Christ, the Blessed Virgin, and other saints, so that after a while no one would any longer even attempt to care for him. The friars' consciences demanded that they not tolerate his blasphemy. Still, they brought the issue to St. Francis, telling him the story of this leprous man. After hearing the whole story, Francis went to see him.

"God's peace be with you, my brother," he said, greeting the man.

The man looked angrily at Francis. "What peace do I have? God has taken everything from me that is good and replaced it with all that stinks!"

"Be patient, my son," Francis began, "for the weaknesses of the body are given to us so that our souls may be saved. They are a great blessing, if you can endure them with more patience."

"How am I supposed to be patient amid constant pain, every day and all night long? And not only am I crucified with this illness, but your friars cannot care for me. Not one knows how to serve me the way he should!"

At this, Francis listened to the Holy Spirit, who told him of the man's troubled spirit, and he went away to pray to God on his behalf. After a while, he returned to him and said, "I want to care for you myself, since you are not happy with any of the others."

"Okay," the man replied, "but what can *you* do for me?"

"I will do whatever you ask."

"I want you to wash me all over my body. I smell so foul that I cannot stand it myself," the leper said.

Francis did as he asked of him. He boiled water and added sweet herbs. He removed the man's clothes and washed his body with his own hands, while one other friar helped by pouring the water.

While Francis did this, touching the man with his own holy hands, the leprosy began to disappear. The leper saw what began to happen and as it did, he grew remorseful for his sins. As the man's flesh was healing, he began to weep, his conscience being baptized by tears as his body was washed with water.

"Oh my soul," he said finally. "I deserve hell for my sins, my impatience and blaspheming." This continued for fifteen days, as the healed leper plumbed the depths of his soul and sought God's mercy through tears, prayer, and confession. Francis observed all of this and knew that it was a miracle that God made happen through his own hands. So before the people of that place could find out what had happened, Francis fled to a distant place, so that he would not be recognized or glorified. Soon thereafter, the healed leper fell ill with another sickness and, enjoying the sacraments of the Church, he died in holiness and peace.

At the very moment that the leper's soul was in the sky, shining like the sun, flying toward heaven, it spoke to Francis, who was at that moment praying. "Do you know me?" the man's soul said.

"Who are you?" Francis replied.

"I'm the leper who was healed by Christ through your good work. Now, I am heading to paradise. I thank you and God for you. And know that every day the angels and saints give thanks to God for the fruit you have produced in the world through your holy Order," he said. And then he disappeared.

[#25 of 53]

CHAPTER 9

Brother Rufino is severely tempted by the devil

[1210 – 1215]

BROTHER RUFINO WAS ONE OF THE NOBLEMEN OF Assisi who became an early companion of St. Francis. He was a saintly man, but was attacked and tempted by the devil while Francis was still alive.

On this occasion, the devil attacked Rufino regarding predestination; he told the friar that he was eternally damned, predestined to that fate, and no matter what he might do was of no use. Rufino listened to this and became very depressed; then he became ashamed to tell Francis what was happening. He simply stopped praying and fasting.

Then the devil took the opportunity to attack him even further. He went after Rufino on the outside, appearing before the friar in the guise of the crucified Christ. The devil said to Rufino, "Brother, why do you pray and fast so much, when you know that you're not even destined for eternal life? You should listen to me, since I know whom I have chosen. Don't believe the son of Peter Bernardone even if he tells you otherwise.*

---

* Peter Bernardone was Francis of Assisi's father. There are occasions in the stories of St. Francis when he accuses himself of arrogance or some other sin by reminding himself that he's simply the son of Bernardone. (See chapter 10.)

In fact, don't even ask him about this, for no one but me knows this information. Even St. Francis is damned. Everyone who follows him is going to hell."

Rufino went completely dark with this news from the devil. He lost his faith completely, and his love for Francis vanished.

But Francis knew what was happening, for the Holy Spirit showed it all to him. He called Brother Masseo and asked him to send Brother Rufino to him. "I will have nothing to do with Brother Francis," Rufino told Masseo.

Masseo could even sense what was happening. He could see the evil enemy at work. "Rufino, Francis is like an angel. He has filled people's souls with the light of God. Come with me to see him, for I can see that you are being deceived," he replied.

And so Rufino followed Masseo to go and see Francis. Seeing him coming from afar, Francis cried out, "Brother! You mischievous one! What is that which you are believing?" And he explained to him what had happened, and how that devil was not at all Christ.

"The next time that the devil tells you how you're damned, you tell him, 'Open up, and I'll crap in your mouth!'" Francis told Rufino. "When you tell him that, he will go. He's doing his job, trying to harden your heart toward what is good; but Christ will give you a soft heart of faith. As Christ says through his prophet: 'A new heart I will give you, and a new spirit I will put within you; and I will remove from your body the heart of stone and give you a heart of flesh.'"*

Rufino began to weep. He was at once comforted by Francis's words and convicted at the same time. "Go to confession, my son," Francis told him. "And get back to your prayers, for temptation will always come again."

So it did, and when Brother Rufino was once back in the woods praying, the enemy returned before him looking like Christ.

"Didn't I tell you, brother, not to believe Bernardone and not to bother praying, because your soul is already damned?" the devil said.

"Open your mouth and I will crap in it!" Rufino shouted at him.

And the devil went away so quickly that it caused an avalanche of rocks from Mount Subasio. The ruckus was so great that Francis and other companions came out of Portiuncula to see what had happened.

The next time that Rufino was devoutly praying, the true Christ appeared before him and Rufino's soul burned with love. "You did well, my son," Christ said, blessing Rufino. "The devil depressed you, but I am your Christ, and from this day forward I will never allow you to be depressed like that." Then he left, and Brother Rufino was left in joy and peace of mind that lasted

---

* Ezekiel 36:26.

both day and night. He was like a new man. And so Brother Francis came to say of Rufino that Christ made him a saint even before he died.[*]

[#29 of 53]

---

[*] See two chapters later: "How St. Francis discerned secrets in the hearts of his companions."

CHAPTER 10

———

Why Brother Rufino has to preach in Assisi in his underwear

[1210 – 1215]

BROTHER RUFINO HAD BECOME SUCH A CONTEMPLATIVE, so constantly absorbed in God, that he never spoke and rarely considered the world outside. He had never had the ability or gift of public speaking. Regardless, St. Francis instructed him one day to go into Assisi and preach to the people with the inspiration of God.

"But father, please excuse me. Don't ask me to do this. As you know, I don't have the gift for preaching," Rufino pleaded with Francis.

"You should have obeyed at once, and since you did not, now I tell you: Go into Assisi wearing only your underwear. Find a church and preach to the people naked!"

And so Rufino did as he was told; he undressed and went in his underwear to find a church in Assisi. First, he knelt before the altar and then he ascended to the pulpit and began to speak.

The people who were there began to twitter with laughter. "They are a bunch of crazy penitents!" someone said.

Now, after Rufino had gone, Francis began to recount in his mind how Rufino had obeyed him. He remembered that Rufino had once been a gentleman of Assisi, and he considered what a difficult thing he had asked him to do. Considering all of this, Francis grew deeply sorry for what he had done. He accused himself, saying, "You are the son of Peter Bernardone. You little wretch! Who are you to order the noble Brother Rufino to go naked and preach like a crazy man?

"You should do to yourself what you make others do," he muttered. And so he did.

Immediately, Francis removed his habit and began to make his way fervently into Assisi. Brother Leo quietly carried the habit, as well as Brother Rufino's, and followed behind. Francis found the church where Rufino was preaching. He heard Rufino saying these words, "Leave the world behind, my friends, and give what belongs to others back to them. Keep God's commandments and love your neighbor. Do penance. Do all of these things for the love of heaven, because God's kingdom is coming soon."

Then Francis climbed into the pulpit. The people began to call him crazy too. But then he began to preach such that the men and women who were there soon began to weep. Before long, with devotion in their hearts, the people began to ask God for mercy, and nearly every listener that day was converted to Christ and turned away from the world. Throughout the town people honored Christ's Passion and it was said that never before had such weeping been heard in Assisi in a single day.

When they were all done, St. Francis put Brother Rufino's habit back on him. Only then did he also get dressed. Wearing their clothes once again, they returned to the Portiuncula thanking God for allowing them to forget themselves long enough to be an example for Christ of how the world is to be left behind.

It was on that day that they first saw people reach to touch the hem of their garments in order to receive a blessing.

[#30 of 53]

CHAPTER 11

———

How St. Francis discerned secrets in the hearts of his companions

[1210 – 1215]

JESUS CHRIST SAYS IN THE GOSPEL, "I AM THE GOOD shepherd. I know my own and my own know me."* Similarly, our Father Francis was like a good shepherd and knew by divine telling what were the qualities, moral decisions, and failings of his companions. With this gift Francis knew how to heal the members of his spiritual family, sometimes recommending a humbling of the proud, and for others, raising up the humble.

On one occasion, St. Francis was sitting at the Portiuncula with his friends talking about God when they noticed that Brother Rufino was not with them. He was still in the woods talking with God alone. But while Francis was talking, that virtuous servant of God, Rufino, returned to the friary. Francis saw him walking by.

"So, brothers," he paused and said to the gathering, "who do you think is the holiest soul in all the world?"

"You," they all responded to Francis.

"No, I am the most unworthy of all men," Francis quickly replied. "Don't you see blessed Brother Rufino

———

* John 10:14.

emerging from those woods? God has shown me how he is one of the three holiest souls living. I would even call him Saint Rufino right now, while he is yet alive."

He said these things to the companions when Rufino was clearly out of range to hear.

But Francis also knew how to be a shepherd who sometimes shows his sheep where they have failed, as he did with Brother Elias when he often accused him of pride, and Brother John of Capella, whose hatred he foresaw would lead him to hang himself. Deeper still, Francis knew the sheep in whom grace overflowed, such as Brother Bernard and Brother Rufino, and many others whose moral failings and virtues he knew by revelation from Jesus Christ. Amen.

[#31 of 53]

CHAPTER 12

Brother Masseo craves the virtue of humility

[1210 – 1215]

ATHER FRANCIS'S EARLIEST COMPANIONS WERE men who were materially poor but wealthy in God. They did not try to obtain things like gold and silver, but instead, with virtues and strength, to persevere toward heaven.

In this spirit, Brother Masseo one day was chatting with St. Francis about God when Francis told him this story:

"There once was a nobleman who was also an intimate friend of God. He had both an active and a contemplative life, and his humility was great to the point that he clearly understood his own sinfulness. He was sanctified and grew by God's grace in all virtue. God looked out for this man and he never fell into sin. . . ."

Now, as Brother Masseo listened to these praiseworthy things, he began to realize that humility itself was the ultimate treasure and that eternal life itself depended upon it. There and then, he vowed never to seek joy in the things of this world, but to pursue the utmost humility in his soul. He made this vow, and then he went to his cell, where he remained the rest of the day, and then for many days on end, fasting, staying awake all night, praying, and weeping to God asking that God might send him to hell for his sins.

This went on until one day when Masseo, in this same spirit of sadness, wandered into the forest. As he cried and sighed to himself and to God, contritely begging God for humility and virtue, a voice from heaven called out.

"Brother Masseo! Brother Masseo!"

"My Lord!" replied Masseo, for he knew that it was Christ who was calling him.

"What will you give me in exchange for all that you desire?" Christ said.

"My very eyes!" Masseo replied.

"But I don't want your eyes," Christ said. "Keep them, and have my grace as well." And with that, the voice was gone.

Masseo was full of joy from that moment forward. He became the humblest of men and took to praying with such joy that he would coo like a pigeon. He always remained in joy-filled contemplation and happiness filled his heart. There was a brother named James of Falerone who once asked Brother Masseo why he was so joyful all the time. "Because when you've found joy and goodness, you never need anything else," he said.

[#32 of 53]

CHAPTER 13

Preaching to the birds

[c a .   1 2 1 0 – 1 2 2 2]

IN THE EARLY DAYS, SOON AFTER HIS HUMBLE CONVERSION and the founding of the movement, St. Francis had great doubts about his vocation. He questioned whether he was called to constant prayer or to preaching—a contemplative or an active life. He wanted to know what would please God the most. So he humbly went to others in order to ask for their help in discerning God's will.

He called Brother Masseo and said, "Go and find Sister Clare and Brother Sylvester and ask them to pray on my behalf to God, and to ask God if I should preach or devote myself entirely to prayer." Masseo did as he was told.

Now Sylvester very often received immediate answers to his prayers, and he did this time as well. He quickly said to Masseo, "Tell Brother Francis this. God has brought him this far so that a harvest of souls will come about as a result. Many people will be saved through him."

Then Masseo went back to Clare, to see if she had received an answer as well. She had. She told Masseo that God told her exactly what he had told Sylvester. At this, Masseo rushed back to Francis. The saint received him with love, washing his feet, preparing food for him to eat after his long walking. And once Masseo had finished eating, Francis asked him to sit with him in the forest outside. He knelt down beside his brother Masseo and said, "What does Jesus want me to do?"

"He wants you to preach wherever you are, for God did not bring you this far for yourself alone, but for the saving of many others."

"All right then, let's go!" Francis replied, leaping to his feet. He grabbed Brother Angelo, and the three ran down the nearest path with a spiritual passion that they didn't even quite understand.

Soon they arrived at Cannara and there, Francis began to preach. Now there were a multitude of swallows in that place who were twittering so loudly that Francis's voice could barely be heard. He asked them to be quiet and they did. The people of Cannara then heard Francis's voice, and saw what the birds did at his command, and many of them wanted to follow him from that moment on.

"Don't hurry away with me now," Francis said. "I will advise you on what to do soon," he said. (From that moment he began to plan for the Third Order.)

Leaving the people of Cannara behind him, he rushed on to Bevagna and there began to preach again until he realized that once again a flock of birds—many kinds—were gathering like an audience to hear him. Francis paused and looked on the birds. He thought of them as his sisters. "Wait for me a moment," he said to his companions. "I am going to preach to *them*." And he walked into the field where the flocks were all gathered in trees above. Upon hearing his voice, and his coming near, they slowly came down to the ground and gathered all around Francis. As he spoke to them, he deliberately touched them, when he could, with the fabric of his habit. Not one of them moved when he did this.

His sermon to the birds was basically this, as recorded by Brother Masseo:

"My little bird sisters, you should praise your Creator because he has given you the gift of flight and freedom, colorful clothing, food and water that you never need to sow, and such beautiful voices. The air is all yours! The mountains and crags and trees are yours! God gives you all that you need. Your Creator loves you. Therefore, always be grateful and praise him."

At these words, the birds stretched their wings, opened their beaks, and moved their heads as if they were making slow bows. It was clear that they heard Francis and appreciated what he had to say. Finally, Francis made the sign of the cross over these creatures and told them that they could leave. At this, they all ascended into the air, in song, forming quickly into four different flocks, flying off to the east, west, south, and north. This signifies that the birds were just like Francis and his first companions. Under the sign of the cross, they flew to the corners of the world, preaching of Christ, possessing nothing of this world, committed entirely to God's will. All of this to the praise of Jesus Christ. Amen.

[#16 of 53]

CHAPTER 14

———

Brother Bernard soars high in contemplation

[1210 – 1225]

ONCE HE TOOK UP THE FRANCISCAN HABIT, Brother Bernard of Quintavalle became known for his soaring contemplation. On one occasion while he was at Mass, he became so absorbed in contemplating divine things that he failed to kneel when the Body of Christ was elevated. He also did not pull his cowl back as the others all did, and he sat completely still, without expression, unaware of anything around him from morning until midafternoon.

After None was over, he returned to his senses.* He then walked all over the friary, shouting to the others, "Brothers! Brothers! There is no man anywhere, no matter how great, no matter how much he was promised in riches, who wouldn't happily carry a bag of dung to win this amazing treasure!"

For fifteen years Bernard went everywhere with his mind and countenance turned like this toward heaven. He never ate until he was satisfied at meals, but would consume as little as was necessary and nothing that tasted good. He also became a man whom the scholars

———

* The liturgical hour known as "None," the ninth hour of prayer (nine hours from the time of dawn), traditionally at about 3 PM.

consulted for help in answering confusing questions and untying the notes of understanding that sometimes come with passages of Scripture.

Because Bernard's mind was free, he soared like a swallow. On occasion, for twenty or thirty days at a time, he would remain on a mountaintop in divine contemplation. For this reason, Brother Giles would sometimes say of Brother Bernard that his gift was so unusual that perhaps he should take his food while flying in the air.

It was because of these graces given to Bernard that St. Francis would often talk with his brother both day and night. They were known to spend an entire evening in contemplation together in the woods, where they had gone to talk about our Lord.

[#28 of 53]

CHAPTER 15

The remarkable life of young Brother Simon

[1 2 1 0 – 1 2 4 4]

IN THE EARLY DAYS OF OUR ORDER, WHILE ST. FRANCIS was still alive, the young Brother Simon joined the movement. God gave him a great amount of grace and peace, raising him to such a level of contemplation that his whole life was like a mirror of all that's holy. People who knew him for many years have told me of all the things that follow.*

Rarely was he seen away from his cell, and if he occasionally went out with other friars, he was always yearning to talk exclusively about God. He had no schooling whatsoever. He loved the woods. He spoke with such depth, so ethereally, that his words were believed to come from some divine place.

On one occasion Brother Simon went into the woods to talk about God with Brother James of Massa.† They spent the entire evening in devout conversation about the love of Christ, and when morning came, they were

---

* This is the first instance where Brother Ugolino refers to himself in the first person, as the narrator of these tales.

† There is a later story devoted to this friar, who some of the prominent friars, such as Brother Giles, believed to be the most holy of them all. See chapter 48, "When God showed Brother James of Massa true secrets."

surprised to realize how long they had been there. I was told of this by one who was present.

Brother Simon used to receive visits from the Holy Spirit and such divine illuminations that he had to lie down as God's love poured over him. That sweet peace of the Spirit made him seem like he was sleeping on his bed. But he was actually caught up in God, resting mentally as well as physically, visited by the divine presence, ignoring any and all material and sensible things.

On one of these occasions, while he was caught up in God and unaware of what was going on around him, one of the other friars desired to test him. The friar took a hot coal from the fireplace and placed it on Simon's uncovered foot. Brother Simon didn't feel anything, showed no pain or suffering or even a wound to the flesh, even though the coal remained on his foot until it had completely burned itself out.

When he would come to take his meals with the other friars, Brother Simon would first give some spiritual food to his companions through divine conversation, before he began to eat what would sustain his own body. So it happened one day that while he was speaking of God with some of the friars, a young man from San Severino* came to the Lord. He'd been

---

* Probably the San Severino that is a municipality in the Marche region of Italy, where many of the Franciscan Spirituals were living in the generations after St. Francis's death. Could this young man be the same person later identified as Brother Masseo of San Severino in chapter 43?

a noble and extremely sensual man in the world, but Simon received him into the Order and gave him the holy habit to replace his secular clothes. This young man remained with Simon to be instructed by him in how to live a religious life.

But the devil hurried in on that young man like a roaring lion, anxious to stop any good work. With every evil breath—the sort of breath that makes coals burn—the devil kindled a burning in the young man's flesh, so much so that he soon gave up hope of resisting temptation.

"Give me my secular clothes back," he said to Brother Simon. "I am under temptations of the flesh that I can no longer resist!"

But Brother Simon looked on him with compassion. "Sit down, son," he said to him, and he proceeded to pour such beautiful words of God into the youth's ears that the flames of temptation and lust melted away in him. Later, when the temptations would return, Simon would always make those desires go away.

But eventually one night the temptations became more than anyone in the world might resist. The young man who was being attacked went to Brother Simon and said, "Give me my clothes back now! I cannot stay any longer!"

"Come and sit down," Brother Simon replied to the troubled youth, and he came and sat beside him. The youth rested his weary, melancholy head on Simon's chest while Simon talked about God. In his pity for the boy, Brother Simon began to lift his eyes to heaven, praying to God with great devotion. Soon he was caught up in God, and then his prayers were answered. By the time Simon returned to his senses, the youth sensed he was completely free of the temptation. It was as if he had never known it, and the damage of those powerful feelings was transformed into a burning of the Holy Spirit. The burning coal of Brother Simon had lit the youth on fire with a love for God and his neighbor.

It was this young man who later went with compassion and courage to the governor to beg mercy on behalf of a criminal who had been captured and sentenced to lose both of his eyes. With tears and prayer he pleaded that his own eye might be plucked out so that the criminal would only have to lose one of his. The governor and his council, seeing charity truly on fire, saw fit to pardon the criminal completely.*

One more story: There was a day when Brother Simon was out praying in the woods, feeling deep consolation from the Lord in his soul, when a flock of rooks began to caw and clamor, disturbing him with their crying. Simon ordered the birds, in the name of Jesus, to go away and never come back. It's beautiful to remember, now, that for

---

* Brother Ugolino might have in mind the remarkable story from the Gospel of Mark 2:1–12 when Jesus heals the paralytic because of the faith of the man's friends (rather than, it seems, from the faith of the paralytic himself).

the last fifty years those birds have never again been seen in that place, or throughout the entire region. I, Brother Ugolino, born in Monte Santa Maria,* stayed myself there for three years and saw that wonder firsthand. It was also well-known among the friars and laypeople of the whole area. Amen.

[#41 of 53]

---

* Monte Santa Maria is now called Montegiorgio. It is south of Ancona in the Marches region.

CHAPTER 16

———

Brother Bernard goes as a holy fool to Bologna

[1211]

S T. FRANCIS AND HIS EARLY COMPANIONS WERE CALLED
by God to bear the cross of Christ in their hearts and
actions. They were called to preach it with words, and
to be before others—in manner of appearance, austerity
of life, actions, and deeds—as men crucified. For this
reason, they took joy in receiving shame and insults for
God rather than the honors and praise of the world that
other men enjoy.

So they walked the world as pilgrims and foreigners,
taking nothing with them but Christ crucified. Because
they were living branches of the "true vine," which is
Christ, they bore "much fruit" in the souls of all those
they won to God.*

It came to pass in the beginning days of the Order that
St. Francis sent Brother Bernard to Bologna to produce
this fruit for God. Taking only holy obedience as his
companion, Bernard made the sign of the cross and left.

In order to be truly conformed to Christ, Bernard went
directly to the public square of that city and sat down
where as many people as possible would see him. He

---

* In this paragraph, for "foreigners" see Exodus 2:22; for "taking nothing" see
Luke 9:3; and for the "true vine . . . much fruit" see John 15:1, 5.

looked the outcast. He knew that he was reproachable in their eyes. And the children were the first to see his unusualness; they began to mock him and make faces as if at a lunatic.

While Bernard sat there in the square, many people gathered around him. Some pulled on his hair. Others threw dirt in his face, and stones. At all of these insults, Bernard remained joyful and persisted there with an expression of contentment. Each day he returned there, and each day he received the same sort of treatment.

After several days, a wise doctor of laws, who had watched what was happening to Brother Bernard and marveled at the virtue of his patience, thought to himself, *Surely this man is some sort of saint.* Finally, he approached Bernard and asked him, "Who are you and where have you come from?"

At this, Bernard simply put his hand in his pocket and pulled out the Rule of St. Francis. He handed it to the learned man. The wise man sat and read it all the way through.* He was amazed at its perfection and impressed by its intelligence. Turning to those that had gathered around him, this doctor of laws said with admiration, "This is the highest form of religious life I have ever encountered! This man and his companions are among the holiest in all the world! Anyone who insults him

---

* The original manuscript of the 1209 Rule has long been lost to history, but it would have been about twenty book pages long.

is committing a sin. This man is a friend of God." And he turned to Brother Bernard and said, "My man, may I give you a place here for prayer, for the sake of my own soul?"

"I think that our Lord himself has inspired you to do so," Bernard answered him. And so the professor led Bernard to his home and then also showed him the place that he had promised to the friars for their work. He furnished it and completed it, all at his expense. And from that day forward, this learned man became a protector in Bologna for the work of Brother Bernard and the Franciscans.

Because of these developments, Brother Bernard quickly became a man of honor in that city, and soon the people there sought to simply see or touch him in order to be blessed. After a while of this, Bernard remembered his lowliness as a follower of the poor man St. Francis, and he departed from there and returned to where Francis was. He said to Francis, "Our place has been founded in Bologna, so you should send friars to maintain and grow it. I am no longer good for that place, myself, for I'm afraid of losing more than I would gain being there."

St. Francis heard all of this, and more of how it had happened, and he rejoiced and gave praise to God.

[#5 of 53]

CHAPTER 17

St. Francis keeps Lent on an island in Perugia

[ca. 1211 – 1215]

IN MANY WAYS, AS A TRUE SERVANT OF JESUS CHRIST, St. Francis was given to the world as Christ himself had been: for its salvation. God's will was accomplished through Francis, as we saw in the lives of the twelve companions, the mysteries of the stigmata, and in the continuous fasting of holy Lent that Francis kept in the following manner.

He was living near the Perugia Lake on Carnival Day, in the home of a friend, when he was inspired to spend Lent on an island in that lake. So he asked his friend to take him in his small craft out into the lake to that island that no one inhabited. He asked the friend to do this quietly on Ash Wednesday, so that no one would notice.

That good friend and follower followed Francis's wish and prepared his little boat in the middle of the night for the short journey. Francis took along only two small loaves of bread.

When the friend was dropping Francis off at the island, Francis begged of him not to mention this to anyone. And he asked him not to return for him until Holy Thursday had come. And so the friend left, and Francis remained.

There were no buildings of any kind on this uninhabited island, and so Francis made a shelter in the midst of some thickets and bushes. There, he began to pray and contemplate divine things. There, he stayed for all of Lent, eating only from those loaves of bread, and drinking nothing at all.

On Holy Thursday, St. Francis's friend returned. The friend found one of the loaves still whole and the other only half-eaten. It is believed that Francis only ate the half in reverence to the fasting of our Lord, who for forty days and forty nights took nothing at all; so Francis took half a loaf in order to avoid the sin of pride, that he might not follow too closely the example of Jesus Christ.

God would later perform many miracles in that place where Francis endured such beautiful abstinence. From that Lent forward, people began to live on that island, and before very long a small town was there. A friary is there now too, and all of the men and women who live in that place know the story of the reverence and devotion of Francis that Lent.

[#7 of 53]

CHAPTER 18

———

St. Francis teaches the wolf and people of Gubbio

[c a . 1 2 1 3 – 1 2 1 6]

A FAMOUS INCIDENT OCCURRED WHILE ST. FRANCIS was living in the town of Gubbio. A fearsome wolf, made crazy with severe hunger, was devouring both animals and human beings.* The people of Gubbio were terrified and took to carrying weapons with them wherever they went. But even weapons did not keep them safe from this wolf. Before long, they stopped going outside the city gates altogether. But God wanted Francis to show the people of Gubbio a better way.

Francis was already there in Gubbio, and so he decided to walk out to meet this wolf. The people said, "Don't do it, Brother Francis! The wolf will kill you, just as it has others before you!"

But Francis put his entire hope in Christ, the ruler of all creatures, and he walked out to meet the wolf armed with nothing but the sign of the cross. A few local people

---

* As with many of the tales in this book, people have contested the factuality of this one. In this case, I find the suggestion fascinating that this wolf may have originally been a man. The Italian word for wolf is *lupo*, and there are local legends that St. Francis converted a criminal in this same region who then became Friar Lupo. We know that a certain Friar Lupo traveled with Francis to Spain. See Raphael Brown, *The Little Flowers of Saint Francis* (New York: Image Books, 1958), 321.

accompanied him for part of the way, but then they said, "This is where we stop."

"You stay here," Francis replied to them, "but I will go on."

A little further on, where the people could still see clearly what was happening, the wolf bounded toward Francis with his mouth gaping. The saint met the wolf making the sign of the cross, and the creature slowed down. It closed its mouth.

"Come here, Brother Wolf," Francis said to it. "In Christ's name, you must not hurt me or anyone else." The wolf came and lay down at the saint's feet.

Francis continued: "Brother Wolf, you have harmed many people and creatures in this place, cruelly destroying and killing. You deserve to be put to death like a murderer would be; but Brother Wolf, I want to make peace between you and the people of Gubbio. You must not harm them, and they will forgive you for your past sins."

The wolf moved its tail and ears and nodded its head.

"Since you agree, I further promise that the people of Gubbio will feed you every day for as long as you live. You will never again go hungry, leading you to commit these crimes of yours. But again—to be sure—I want you to promise that you will never hurt any creature. Will you?" Francis asked.

The wolf nodded in clear assent.

"Give me a pledge of your agreement to this," Francis said. And the wolf held out its paw, putting it in Francis's outstretched hand.

"So then come with me now, to seal this pact with the people themselves," Francis said. And the wolf walked beside Francis like a lamb into the town of Gubbio until they reached the market square where all of the people had assembled. There, Francis preached a sermon. He said that God allows awful things to happen sometimes because of our sins, and that the fire of hell is far worse than the dangers posed by a hungry wolf. A wolf may be able to kill our bodies, but hell is something truly frightful. And one simple animal shouldn't be able to keep a people in a constant state of fear and trembling. "So come back to God," he said, "and do penance for these sins of yours, and God will bring freedom to both you and this wolf now and in the next world."

Then Francis announced: "Brother Wolf has promised to be peaceful with you. He will no longer harm you. And I have told him that you will provide him with food every day. I stand between you today as we all make this pact." And then the people in one voice agreed to what they had heard.

And Francis turned and said to Brother Wolf, "Do you agree?" The wolf bowed his head and wagged his tail so that everyone there could see. He raised his paw once again and placed it in the hand of Francis. The crowd from Gubbio was amazed at all of this and they shouted praises to God for bringing Francis to their part of the world. From that day forward, the people of Gubbio and the wolf of Gubbio lived together in peace. For two years, Brother Wolf was fed by each house in the town. He harmed no one. Not a single dog ever barked at his comings and goings. Then the wolf died of old age and the people of Gubbio were actually sorry to see their symbol of peace and kindness go.

[#21 of 53]

CHAPTER 19

The haughtiness of Brother Elias

[c a . 1 2 1 3 A N D c a . 1 2 1 9]*

I N THE BEGINNING DAYS OF THE ORDER, when there were few friars and their houses had not yet been established, St. Francis took a pilgrimage with some of his companions, including Brother Bernard. They traveled on the road to St. James of Compostela.†

Along the Way of St. James, they came across a sick young man in one of the villages. Francis felt compassion for him and said to Brother Bernard, "My son, I'd like you to stay behind and care for him." Bernard quickly agreed and kneeled before Francis in humility, showing that he would obey in obedience to his father. He stayed behind while the others continued on to Compostela.

Arriving at the Church of St. James, they spent the night in prayer. While there, Francis received a revelation showing him that he needed to found many places where Franciscans would reside throughout the world. The

---

* This story contains two sets of approximate dates because the trip of St. Francis to Spain (at the outset) took place in 1213, but the lesson of the latter portion of the tale, where a rule is imposed on the friars not to eat meat, didn't take place until 1219 or later.

† Tradition has it that St. James the Great, one of Jesus' twelve apostles, is buried in northwestern Spain, and the pilgrimage to that place, known as Santiago de Compostela, was one of the most popular destinations throughout the Middle Ages.

Order he'd founded was intended to spread into a great multitude. And then they left St. James and returned the way that they had come. They came eventually back to the place where Brother Bernard had stayed behind with the sick man. The man had recovered fully from his illness, and Francis invited Bernard to travel the Way of St. James the following year.

Meanwhile, Francis returned to the valley of Spoleto,* and he and Brother Masseo and Brother Elias and some others went into the woods to pray. Now Francis's companions usually left him alone at these times, as they were afraid to disturb what God might have to say to their father in moments of quiet. But one day, while Francis was at prayer, a handsome young man came to the door of where they were all staying and knocked loudly and rapidly. The friars were surprised by the intrusion. Brother Masseo finally went to the door and opened it, saying, "Where are you from, boy? You've obviously never been here before, or you wouldn't knock so rudely!"

"How is one supposed to knock, then?" the young man said.

"Knock three times," Masseo replied, "and slowly. In fact, then wait for as long as it might take a friar to say an Our Father. And even then, if a friar hasn't yet come, knock quietly once again."

---

* A geographical phrase used to mean the place where the Portiuncula is located. See also chapter 23.

"Well, I'm in a hurry," the man responded, "and I knocked that way because I need to see Brother Francis. He's in the woods praying and I don't want to disturb him—so perhaps you could send Brother Elias to help me, for I have a question and I have heard that he is wise."

Brother Masseo left the doorway and went to Brother Elias, asking him if he would speak with the young man. But Elias was proud and angry and he refused to go.

Masseo didn't then know what to do or what to say to the young man. If he said, *Brother Elias can't come just now*, he'd be lying, but if he told the man the truth, the man would see a bad example. While Masseo pondered these options, the young man knocked again, and just as he had the first time. At that, Masseo returned to the gate and said, "You didn't knock the way I told you to!"

The man replied to Masseo: "Brother Elias will not come, so go and tell Brother Francis that I have come, but since I don't want to interrupt his prayers, ask him to send Elias to me." Masseo did as he was told by this man, who he now realized was an angel.

Masseo went to the woods and found Francis with his face lifted up toward heaven. Without moving, Francis said, "Go tell Brother Elias to go to the young man immediately, as an act of obedience."

When Elias heard Francis's order for him, he was furious. He stomped to the gate and flung open the door, exclaiming, "What do you want!?" The man answered him, "Be careful of anger, brother, because it can darken the soul and cloud the mind."

"What do you want from me!?" Elias demanded again.

"I have come to ask you a question. Is it lawful for followers of the holy Gospel to eat whatever is set before them, as Christ taught? Similarly, is it lawful for any person to impose on followers of the holy Gospel anything that is contrary to its freedoms?"

Brother Elias answered haughtily. "I know these answers very well, but I won't tell you. Go away." He threw the gate closed and left.

But after he'd left the man's presence, Brother Elias began to ponder the questions. He realized that he was unsure of the answers—for he himself had made a rule for the friars, when he was vicar of the Order, that no one was allowed to eat meat. Perhaps that question had been aimed directly at him? Unable to make sense of it all, and recalling how humble the man at the gate had been, Elias returned there and looked for him again. The man wasn't there. Elias searched all around the friary and he was nowhere to be found. The angel had left, for Brother Elias was unfit to speak with the angels.

Once all of this had occurred, St. Francis (who knew of it all) returned from the woods. He found Brother Elias and scolded him, saying, "Only a too-proud friar would drive away a holy angel, who only wanted to teach us something, from this place. I fear that your haughtiness will lead you to end your days outside of this Order." It would later happen just as Francis had predicted.

Meanwhile, on the same day and hour as the angel had left the gate before Brother Elias, he appeared to Brother Bernard, who was returning from the Way of St. James. Bernard was standing on the bank of a river, unable to cross it. The angel greeted Bernard in words that he could easily understand, saying, "Peace be with you, brother."

Brother Bernard was amazed at the handsomeness of the man and his eloquence and peacefulness. He said to him, "Where are you from, young man?"

The angel replied, "I have come from where St. Francis is living, and I went to see him, but was unable to, because he is in the woods with God. Brothers Masseo, Giles, and Elias were there, too, and Masseo taught me the proper way to knock at the gate, the way good friars do. And Elias—not wanting to answer the question that I put to him—then had regret and wanted to see me again, but couldn't.

"Why won't you cross the river?" the angel concluded.

"I am afraid of how deep it is here," Bernard answered him.

"Let's pass over together," the angel said. "There's no need for fear." And he took Bernard's hand. In a flash of a moment, they were standing together on the other side. At this, Brother Bernard knew he was in the presence of an angel. With joy and reverence he shouted out, "O blessed angel of God, tell me, what is your name?"

"It is wonderful," the man said, "but tell me, why do you need to know?" And at that, he disappeared.

Brother Bernard was left in happiness and joyfully continued his journey all the way home to St. Francis and the other brothers. He told them of what had happened, including the very hour when the angel came to him, and they all knew that it was the same angel who had come to the brothers and to Bernard on that very same day. They gave thanks to God.

[#4 of 53]

CHAPTER 20

St. Francis shows special care for some wild birds

[c a .   1 2 1 5 – 1 2 2 0]

ONE DAY A BOY IN SIENA CAUGHT SOME TURTLEDOVES and carried them, still fluttering about, to the market. St. Francis, who was always compassionate to creatures, and especially to animals and birds, saw these turtledoves and his heart was moved.

"Will you give these birds to me?" he asked the young boy. "They are innocent creatures that the Bible says are pure and faithful souls. Give them to me so that they don't go to anyone who will kill them."

The boy was inspired by God and Francis's words and he agreed. So Francis gathered up the turtledoves and began talking with them in gentle tones.

"My sisters," he said, "why did you allow yourselves to be captured like this? You are innocent. You need nests where you can lay eggs and multiply as your Creator has instructed you."

With this, Francis took the birds to a place where he then made nests for each of them. And the doves settled down into those nests and began to lay eggs in that place, where the friars also lived. Over time, they became so tame with the men that they were almost like chickens that had been raised from chicks by the brothers. They would even come and go when Francis would bless them.

Back at the market, St. Francis had said to that boy, "You will surely serve our Lord Jesus Christ and become a Friar Minor someday." And so it happened that the youth soon entered the Order. The actions of Francis led to life and joy for some turtledoves, but also to the joy of eternal life for the boy who gave them to him. Christ be praised. Amen.

[#22 of 53]

CHAPTER 21

When St. Francis saw the Portiuncula surrounded by devils

[ca. 1215–1220]

ONCE AT PORTIUNCULA, WHILE ST. FRANCIS WAS fervently praying, a vision showed him that the entire place was surrounded by an army of devils. At the same time, he saw that none of the devils could enter the friary on its own; it needed a holy friar to allow it inside. And so—as he watched—they waited.

The next moment, one of the friars in the Portiuncula became stirred up with anger against one of the others. He began to contemplate how to get revenge against his brother. As a result, the gate of virtue briefly fell and a door to evil was opened; a devil found his way inside that place.

Seeing all of this, Francis then watched as that devil crouched itself upon that friar's neck. It was as if a wolf were devouring one of his sheep. Francis called out for the friar, and the man came running to Francis, who instructed him to reveal what was going on between him and his neighbor. The friar, seeing that his spiritual father had "read" his very thoughts, revealed everything to Francis that he had been hiding darkly in his heart, asking humbly for forgiveness. Francis listened to him, and gave him a penance, absolving the man of his sin.

At that moment, the father watched as his son's devil flew away. Christ be praised.

[#23 of 53]

CHAPTER 22

A rich and noble knight becomes a Franciscan friar

[1215 – 1220]

S T. FRANCIS AND HIS COMPANIONS ARRIVED **very late** one evening at the house of a venerable gentleman. They were treated with courtesy, reverently given a resting place for the night—so much so that they were made to feel like angels arriving from heaven. The nobleman embraced Francis with a kiss of peace and washed his feet, kissing them too. He lighted a warm fire and set a table of many foods, serving the friars by his own hand, and with joy. These extraordinary kindnesses warmed Francis's heart.

"Father," the nobleman asked Francis, when the meal was done, "I offer you all that I have. And if you need to purchase anything—habits or clothing or anything else—buy it and I will repay you. I want to provide for your needs out of my abundance."

And so, later, when Francis was leaving this man's house with his companions, he remarked to them, "That nobleman would make an excellent member of our Order. Someday, I would like to return here and find that God has touched him further, making him want to join us in serving God. Let's pray that God might further spark his heart by that grace."

A few days later, St. Francis said to one of his companions, "Let's go back to the noble gentleman's house because I feel that God has worked in his heart." And so they took to the road that led to the man's house, but before they could arrive at his door, Francis said to his brother, "Wait here for me. I want to ask God to make our journey a success. I want to ask Christ to give those of us who are weak the ability to snatch strong prey away from the world!" Saying this, he went off in private to pray—but not so privately that he couldn't be seen clearly by the gentleman himself.

The gentleman saw Francis devoutly praying to Christ; and he saw Christ himself standing with Francis beautifully enwrapped in a bright light. Francis was even rising off the ground—both spiritually and physically.

The hand of God came upon the gentleman as he viewed these happenings, touching his heart and inspiring him to leave the world completely behind. He left his mansion and ran to St. Francis. There he found Francis still standing in prayer, and so he too began to pray, and then he knelt before Francis and pleaded with him to show him the way to penance and to join him permanently.

"What should I do, father?" the man said to Francis. "I am ready to give everything to those in need and to run with you after Christ."

This is how it happened that such a nobleman became a Friar Minor and gave all that he had to the poor.

[#37 of 53]

CHAPTER 23

———

A general chapter is held at St. Mary of the Angels

[1216 or 1218]

CHRIST'S FAITHFUL SERVANT ST. FRANCIS OF ASSISI
once held a general chapter of the early Franciscans
in the valley below Assisi at St. Mary of the Angels.*
More than 5,000 friars were there. While traveling
from Bologna to Rome, St. Dominic, the founder of the
Order of Friars Preachers, along with seven of his friars,
heard of this gathering and they went to see what was
happening.

Also there was Lord Ugolino, the cardinal bishop
of Ostia, who was always devoted to Francis and his
brothers. Francis once prophesied that the cardinal
bishop would be pope one day, and so it happened, when
he became Pope Gregory IX. But during this general
chapter, Lord Ugolino's court was in Perugia and he came

---

* James of Vitry, a theologian, cardinal, and historian who lived at the
time of St. Francis, wrote in a letter dated 1216, after traveling to see
the Franciscans firsthand in Italy: "The men of this religious order gather
once a year in a chosen place, to their great benefit, that they might dine
together and rejoice in the Lord. They get the advice of worthy men
and they decide on and then promote and get papal approval for holy
projects. After this they disperse for the whole year. . . . I am convinced
that the Lord . . . wishes before this world comes to an end to save many
souls through these simple and poor men." (Quoted in *Religious Poverty and
the Profit Economy in Medieval Europe*, by Lester K. Little [Ithaca, NY: Cornell
University Press, 1978], 151.)

often to Assisi, sometimes every day, singing the Mass, and sometimes delivering sermons for the friars.

The cardinal was inspired by the sight of this holy assembly of brothers sitting in the plain below Assisi. They were in groups of sixty or one hundred, or more, just talking about God, praying with one another, crying with each other, and doing acts of charity. This was a quiet and humble army of men, making no unnecessary noise, telling no stories, making no jokes, but only praying the Divine Office and talking about the salvation of human souls. They slept on the ground or on a pile of straw, and their pillows were stones or logs.

"This is certainly a camp of the knights of God!" the cardinal exclaimed.

Everyone who saw this gathering of men was impressed by their devotion and holiness. Throughout the valley of Spoleto, people came to witness what was happening, including many of the cardinal's court, barons and other noblemen, bishops and abbots. They came to see St. Francis, the one who had brought together such a gathering—who had plucked these men from out of the world and started such a movement of those who followed the true shepherd, Christ. People said that this was unlike any gathering of men ever before assembled.

When they were all assembled, Francis stood before them as minister-general and preached God's Word as the Holy Spirit directed him. His sermon centered on this theme: "My sons, we have received many good things, but greater things are promised to us by God. Let us use the good things all around us, but even more, let's confidently pursue the promises of God. Our life here on earth is short, and the punishment of eternity is real; suffering here and now is nothing, and the glory of heaven is forever."* He counseled and inspired the friars, encouraging them to live faithfully in the life to which they were committed—pursuing humility, patience, contempt for the values of the world, voluntary poverty, care, attentiveness, prayer, and praise. He asked them to put their faith entirely in the Good Shepherd who cares for all of our needs, body and soul. He went on to say: "In order to learn these lessons here and now I say that none of us shall worry about what we will eat or drink or anything else necessary for our bodies, while we are here in this place together. Let's focus only on praying and praising our Lord. Leave all bodily worries to Christ, who cares for us."

They cheered at this, and with joy. And when he had finished speaking, they rushed back to praying together.

Now St. Dominic was there, and expressed his surprise at this command of St. Francis. It might work for one friar, but for a huge group? But before long, the people of the surrounding towns—Perugia, Spoleto, Foligno, Spello, Assisi, and beyond—began delivering food and drink, bread and wine, beans and cheese, to the huge and holy

---

* Perhaps his text was Romans 8:14–18.

congregation of men. On mules and horses they arrived with pitchers and glasses, tablecloths and other utensils, whatever was needed. Then the knights and noblemen began serving the friars. The clergymen were running here and there like servants, for the sake of the brothers. When Dominic saw all of this, he realized that God was at work and he took back what he had previously said. Dominic knelt before the saint himself and said, "God is the one caring for this holy assembly. I didn't see it at first. I now promise to observe holy poverty myself, and all of the men in my Order will do the same!"

It was during that same general chapter that Francis discovered that many of the friars were wearing metal cilices on their torsos and iron rings on their arms, and as a result were becoming ill or even dying. These objects actually hindered rather than helped prayer. So Francis, the wise father, commanded all the brothers to remove these things. They did, and more than five hundred pieces were thrown into a large pile.

When the chapter was ending, Francis asked the brothers to do good in the world and to escape evil, and he sent them back to the many places from which they'd come. May Christ be blessed! Amen.

[#18 of 53]

CHAPTER 24

———

St. Francis takes a ship to see the Sultan

[1 2 1 9]

ST. FRANCIS WAS ZEALOUS IN HIS FAITH TO THE POINT of desiring a martyr's death. One day he took with him twelve of his companions and traveled across the seas to the place of the Sultan* of Babylonia. When they arrived, the Saracen men who protected the roads so that Christians could not travel freely, took them as prisoners, bound and beat them, and then brought them before the Sultan.

There in the Sultan's presence Francis preached by the power of the Holy Spirit. He spoke beautifully of the Catholic religion and even offered to step into a fire to demonstrate his faith. The Sultan admired both his fervor and his distaste for the things of this world—for in his poverty Francis would not accept gifts from the hands of the Sultan. The Sultan also respected Francis's desire for martyrdom. He listened carefully to Francis's words, and asked him to return several times to see him and talk some more. He also gave Francis permission to preach wherever and whatever he chose, giving him and

———

* Famously, St. Francis met with Malik al-Kamil (1180–1238), the Sultan of Egypt, at a time when Christian crusaders were preparing an attack on the Nile Delta region that he ruled. Entire books have been written about this episode. See "For Further Reading."

his holy companions a token of himself so that no one would ever do them any harm.

And so, with permission, Francis sent his companions out in pairs throughout the Saracen lands to preach the faith of Jesus. He himself left with a brother and traveled to a region where they found an inn in which to stay overnight. There Francis found a beautiful woman, who was nevertheless undesirable of soul. She asked Francis to go to bed with her.

"If you will do what I want, I will do what you want," Francis replied.

"Okay," she said, "then let's go and prepare a bed." And she led Francis to a bedroom.

But then Francis said, "Come with me. I will show you a most beautiful bed." And he showed her into a room with a large fire roaring in a fireplace. Stripping himself naked, Francis rushed to climb into the fire as if he was leaping into bed. He called to the woman and said, "Undress yourself. Come and enjoy this wonderful bed! You must come here in order to do what I wanted." And he lay there for a long while without the fire burning him at all. The woman was terrified and felt sorry for her sins and intentions. At that moment, she was converted to faith in Christ.

After a while, however, Francis saw that he and his friars would be unable to gather much fruit in this faraway land, and God told him to go home. He returned to the Sultan and told him of their intention to leave.

"Brother, I myself would gladly convert to your faith, but I am afraid," the Sultan said. "If I were to do so, these Saracens would kill both of us, plus your companions. And since you still have much good to do, and I too have things to do for my own soul, I don't want to cause our deaths too soon. Show me what I might do for salvation, and I will obey."

Francis replied, "My lord, I leave you now to return to my country. But when the time for my death has come, and I am gone to heaven, I will send two of my friars back to you and they will bring you the baptism of Jesus Christ, and you will be saved. In the meantime, do not let anything hinder your desires for faith, and when grace comes, God will find you with faith."

The Sultan promised to do as Francis suggested, and the saint left.

After some years, Francis's body died. And then, when the Sultan became ill, he remembered the saint's promise to him, and he stationed guards at all gates with instructions to inform him if any of Francis's friars were ever seen. It was at this time that Francis appeared to two of his friars and told them what to do.

When the Sultan glimpsed them from afar, he was filled with joy. "I now know that God has saved me, just as Saint Francis had promised," he said. And after receiving some instruction in the faith of Christ, those friars baptized the Sultan, and his soul was saved.

[#24 of 53]

CHAPTER 25

———

Brother Bernard's humility

[ca. 1220]

THE DEVOUT SERVANT OF CHRIST CRUCIFIED, St. Francis, had lost his sight. Nearly blind from all of his severe penances and tears, he set out one day to find Brother Bernard, to speak with his friend. Brother Bernard was adept with words, and Francis loved to talk with him about spiritual things.

When Francis approached the place where Bernard was staying,* he found that Bernard was off in the woods, completely absorbed in prayer and contemplation, united with the Holy One. Francis called his friend, saying, "Come and talk with this blind man!"

Bernard did not answer him or even stir, for his soul was completely lifted up to God at that moment. So Francis called out in the same manner for a second time. And then a third time: "Come and talk with this blind man!"

But Brother Bernard could not hear him at all. So Francis went away with disappointment in his heart, complaining to himself that his brother must not want to speak with him.

———

* This may have been the Carceri hermitages, caves where early Franciscans, including Francis on occasion, lived on the slopes of Mount Subasio just outside of Assisi.

While Francis was on his way, returning from where he'd come, he said to the companion at his side, "Wait here for a short minute!" And he dashed over to a quiet and solitary place to pray, begging God to reveal to him why Bernard had ignored his calling out to him.

A voice came to Francis that said, *Why are you troubled, poor little man? Should a man leave me for one of my creatures? When you were calling, Brother Bernard was united with me. Don't fret that he didn't respond to you. He didn't even hear you.*

At this, Francis dashed back to the place where Bernard was, to humbly accuse himself of what he had been thinking about Bernard and his motives.

Bernard saw Francis coming toward him and ran to greet him, throwing himself down at his feet. Francis quickly made him get up, and he told him what had happened, and ended by saying, "In holy obedience, I ask you to do what I now command of you."

Brother Bernard was wary of this, for Francis was known to be excessive at such moments. So Bernard replied, "I am ready, father, but only if you also promise to also do what I say."

"I agree," Francis said.

"Then say what you want of me, father," Bernard offered.

Francis began: "To punish the presumptions of my heart, I ask you to step on my mouth and my throat three times, while I lie on the ground. And while stepping on me, you should mock me, saying, 'You just lie there, you simple peasant, you son of Peter Bernardone!' And then you must insult me even further, and say, 'Where did you get such pride, since you are worth nothing at all!'"

Now when Brother Bernard heard this, he swallowed hard. But because of holy obedience, he sort of did what was asked of him. But he did it all rather courteously. When Bernard was done, Francis said, "Now, Brother Bernard, order me as you will, because I too have made a promise to obey."

"By like obedience, I ask that you correct me of my faults whenever we are together," Bernard replied.

But Francis marveled at this, for it was difficult for Francis to see many faults in his friend. As a result, from this moment forward, Francis was careful to avoid spending too much time with Brother Bernard, he so wanted to avoid having to point out any faults at all to him. Whenever he desired to speak with Bernard about spiritual things, he was quick to arrive and quick to leave him.

It was always inspiring to watch the affection and love that Francis had for this firstborn son of his. To the praise and glory of Jesus. Amen.

[#3 of 53]

CHAPTER 26

———

St. Clare joins St. Francis for a meal, and the sisters are relieved!

[c a .   1 2 1 0 – 1 2 2 5] *

S T. FRANCIS OFTEN VISITED ST. CLARE WHEN HE WAS
in Assisi, stopping to talk with her for a while. But
after some time, Clare asked Francis for more than these
brief encounters. She wanted the consolation of joining
her friend for a meal. Several times she asked him if they
could eat together, and several times Francis refused.

After some time, Francis's brothers took note of Clare's
desire and disappointment and said to him, "It seems
to us that this strictness of yours is running counter to
divine love. Sister Clare, who has done so much for the
sake of Christ, as a response to your preaching, asks a
simple favor. You should grant it, and then some!"

"If it seems so to you," Francis replied, "then I will do it.

"But let's have this meal at St. Mary of the Angels, for
Clare has been cloistered at San Damiano for a very long
time. She will like seeing the place where her hair was
cut and she was made a spouse of Christ!"

On the appointed day, Clare arrived at St. Mary of
the Angels. She reverently greeted the Blessed Virgin at

———

* Clare formally joined the Franciscan movement as its first woman on
March 18, 1212. Soon afterward, Francis arranged for San Damiano to
become a convent, and Clare lived there for the rest of her four-plus
decades, leaving the grounds rarely and only for a few hours at a time.

the altar, remembering that very place where long before she had taken her vows. The brothers chatted with her. Francis prepared the table—upon the floor—which was his custom. And then it was time to eat.

Francis and Clare sat together, and during that first course, Francis began to speak about God with sensitive holiness and reverence. It seemed to everyone present—Francis, Clare, Clare's companion, the brothers—that a rapturous grace surrounded them.

Outside the Portiuncula, it appeared to the people of Assisi and Bettona* that St. Mary's and the entire forest that then surrounded the chapel were aflame. The men of those towns rushed to the place where they thought a fire was blazing, but when they arrived they saw nothing on the outside, no evidence of fire at all. So they went inside, where they found Francis and Clare and the others in deep contemplation. It was at that moment that they knew this had been a heavenly thing.

Later that evening, when everyone inside returned to themselves, they realized how refreshed and nourished they felt beyond all measure. They looked at the table before them and realized that they'd barely touched the food. Clare returned to San Damiano, thankful.

Meanwhile, her sisters were overjoyed to see her. For they had been afraid that Francis might decide to send her to be abbess in some far-off place, as he'd done earlier with their Sister Agnes.   [#15 of 53]

---

* This ancient Umbrian commune is seven miles southwest of Assisi.

CHAPTER 27

The boy who faints when he sees St. Francis talking with Christ

[c a .   1 2 2 0 – 1 2 2 5]

A CERTAIN PURE AND SIMPLE BOY WAS RECEIVED INTO the Order while St. Francis was still alive, and the boy lived among the brothers when because of voluntary poverty they slept on the ground.

One day, Francis arrived in the evening after saying Compline, and wanted to rest before the others so that he could rise to pray again while they slept. He often did this.

The simple boy decided to observe what Francis did and where he went that night, to spy on his holiness. So to insure that he didn't sleep past when Francis awoke, the boy lay down beside Francis, after he fell asleep, and tied the cord of his tunic to that of Francis.

During the night, when the other brothers were fast asleep, Francis woke up and quickly realized that his cord was tied to the lad's. He gently untied it in a way that the boy could not feel his presence. Then, the saint went outside to the forest where he began to pray alone in a small hut. Before too long, the boy woke up on his own and realized what had happened. Francis was gone. So he too quickly rose, in order to go and find the holy father. The boy went out and discovered that the gate toward the forest lay open—so he went in that direction. Soon he found the saint.

The boy approached Francis very slowly. He stood back at a certain distance. But soon, he heard a multitude of voices. He crept slowly closer, and soon he thought he saw a beautiful light surrounding Francis. Within that light the boy saw Jesus Christ, the Blessed Virgin Mary, John the Baptist, the evangelist known as John, and a company of angels, all of them in conversation with Francis. Seeing all of this, the boy trembled and then he fainted, out cold right there on the path from the monastery to the forest.

A little while later, once the mystery and holy conversation was over, while the boy still lay in the middle of the path, Francis nearly stumbled on top of him while walking back to where the brothers were sleeping. He looked on the lad with compassion and took him up in his arms, carrying him back to that place. In the morning, the boy told Francis what he thought he'd seen and Francis said, "Do not tell anyone, at least as long as I live." The boy did as he was told and kept this secret until after the saint's death.

[#17 of 53]

CHAPTER 28

The problem in the vineyard of the parish priest of Rieti

[c a .   1 2 2 0 – 1 2 2 5]

O N ONE OF THE OCCASIONS WHEN ST. FRANCIS was suffering because of his eyes, the protector of his order, Cardinal Ugolino, wrote to Francis out of love, telling him to come to Rieti to see a physician. Francis received the letter and went first to San Damiano to see St. Clare, the devout bride of Christ; he wanted to see her before he left for Rieti.

At San Damiano, his eyes became worse. The first night he spent there, he could not see a thing. And so Clare had a cell prepared for him, using reeds and straw, a place where he could be alone and rest. Francis ended up staying there for fifty days in great pain. He was also disturbed by the mice that infested the place. Soon he came to realize that the Lord was punishing him for his past sins. He reached out to God in thankfulness and praise, saying, "I deserve this, Lord, and then some. Good Shepherd, you have shown your mercy in the past; now, help your little lamb have the strength to remain by your side no matter what comes!"

A voice came to Francis from heaven, saying, "Answer me this: If the earth were entirely golden, and the oceans of the earth were balsam, and the mountains were all precious gems, would you still be able to conceive of a treasure more valuable than these? And if that most valuable treasure were given to you as an illness, would you be happy about it?"

"I am not worthy of such a thing," Francis replied.

The voice continued: "Then rejoice, brother, because I am keeping this treasure—it is eternal life—as yours, and your current illness is but a pledge of that gift."

At this word, Francis jumped for joy and called for his companion. "Let's get going to Rieti, to see the cardinal!"

When they were approaching Rieti, a crowd of people wanting to meet him began to gather. They were so numerous that Francis wanted to avoid the city, and so they stopped at a church about two miles outside of town. But soon, the people knew what they had done, and they came there to see the saint camping out in a vineyard nearby that was owned by the priest of the little church. It was grape-harvesting time, and all of the grapes were sure to be ruined under the feet, or eaten by the hands, of those throngs of people. When the priest viewed the damage, he regretted ever allowing Francis to enter his church. These thoughts were revealed to Francis by the Spirit of God.

So Francis asked the priest to come and see him. "Father," he said, "how much wine does your vineyard produce in a good year?"

"Twelve measures," he answered.

"Then please," Francis said, "be patient with these people and allow them to stay. Allow them to take whatever they need. And I promise, for the love of God, that your vineyard will produce twenty measures this year."

The priest listened to this promise of Francis and allowed the people to eat whatever they chose. It was a wonderful sight—the vineyard being stripped and ruined by the throngs, for Francis saw that God was doing great things in the souls of the people. Many of them were going away drunken with love for God, turning away from the things of the world, and discovering more heavenly desires.

When all was done, only a few bunches of grapes were left on the vines. But still, the priest ordered that the remaining grapes be gathered and pressed and, as Francis had said, twenty measures resulted that year.

[#19 of 53]

CHAPTER 29

———

Three murderous robbers become Franciscan friars

[c a. 1 2 2 0 – 1 2 2 5]

THE BLESSED FRANCIS WAS ALWAYS TRAVELING, seeking to tell men and women of the way to salvation. Everywhere he traveled he was guided by the Holy Spirit, and made new family members. He spread God's grace to Slavonia, the Marches of Trevisi and Ancona, Apulia, the land of the Saracens, and other provinces, making followers of Christ wherever he went.

On one occasion, while he was traveling through Monte Casale,* a young nobleman of great refinement stopped St. Francis in order to speak with him. "Father," he said, "I would like to become one of your followers."

"My son, you are too young, and too noble, for us. Would you truly be able to endure a life of poverty and difficulty?" Francis replied.

"You are men just like me," the noble young man said. "What you can endure, I can endure."

Francis liked this answer very much, and named him Brother Angelo, and within a short amount of time Angelo was made guardian† of the region of Monte Casale by St. Francis.

---

* A mountainous region in Sicily.

† Franciscans have always used the name "guardian" to refer to what other orders refer to as abbots or superiors.

Now in this time there were three infamous robbers roaming the countryside, and one day they came to where the friars of Monte Casale were residing. They asked Brother Angelo to feed them, and Angelo answered angrily, "You not only rob and murder, but you want to take what has been donated for feeding God's servants! You don't even deserve to be alive! Go somewhere else to insult the God who created you! Don't come back here!"

They went away, but they were furious.

Later that same day, Francis returned to Monte Casale, carrying bread and wine that he had begged along the way. When he arrived, Angelo told him what had happened and how he had successfully driven away the three infamous men. But Francis scolded Angelo.

"You acted cruelly. Sinners will come back to their God by humility, not by scolding. Christ tells us that those who are well do not need a physician, but those who are sick do.

"You acted uncharitably," he continued. "For that, I command you to take this bread and wine and find those three men somewhere in these mountains. Offer it to them. Kneel before them and ask their forgiveness. Then ask them—using my name—to stop doing what they have been doing, to fear the Lord, and no longer harm their neighbors. If they will do this, promise them that we will give them the food and drink that they need, always. Then come back here to me."

Angelo went out to do what he had been commanded by Francis. And Francis prayed earnestly that it would succeed and that God would soften those robbers' hearts.

Before too long, Angelo found the men, gave them the provisions, and told them all that Francis had instructed him to say. The men accepted the gifts and while they were eating, began to talk to one another.

"You know, terrible things await us in hell," one said. "We don't fear men or God and probably have no conscience left at all. And look at this holy friar," he continued, "who brought us food and wine, a promise from his holy father, and all because of a few words that he said to us about our wickedness."

"You're right," the other two said, "but so what?"

The first man spoke again. "Let's go and see St. Francis. If he gives us hope and tells us that God's mercy is possible even for us, than let's do what he says and free our souls from certain hell." The others agreed, and they all left hastily.

When they arrived, they said to Francis, "Father, we don't believe that we can ever receive God's mercy, but if you think it's possible, we're ready to do penance and obey you in whatever you command."

Francis welcomed them with open arms and love. He told them the truth: that God would show his mercy to them, and that Jesus Christ came into the world in order to redeem sinners just like them. As a result, these three robbers renounced their evil and the world and he opened the Franciscan Order to them. For their part, the men began their great penance.

Before long, two of the robbers died and went to heaven, while the third man lived for fifteen more years, doing penance all the while. He kept the usual forty-day fasts that the other friars did, plus he ate only bread and water three days every week. He never owned more than one habit, he walked about barefoot, and he never went to bed after Matins.* During those fifteen years, St. Francis also transitioned from this world to the next.

Then one night, temptation came to the friar who remained. He was tempted to fall asleep after the Matins prayers had ended. He resisted and resisted until finally he could no longer and yielded to temptation. The friar lay down to sleep. That moment—as his head touched the pillow—he began to dream.

He was led up to a mountaintop that looked down on a deep valley. There were jagged rocks on both sides, and he was frightened as he glanced downward. The angel that accompanied him to the mountain suddenly then pushed him over the edge, and he fell headlong into the ravine, his body ricocheting off the rocks and ledges until he struck the bottom floor. As he lay there, he was

---

* Matins is the name for the first prayer time of the day. It was usually scheduled for the hour before the sun's rising.

certain that his bones and limbs were shattered to pieces. At that moment, the angel called down to him, "Get up! You still have a long journey!"

"You are cruel," the friar responded, "for can't you see that I am in pieces?"

So the angel came down to him and touched him. At that moment, the friar was healed. He was one piece again.

Then the angel pointed the direction where the friar must continue on his journey—through a field of thorns, briars, and swamp. He told the friar that he must walk barefoot until he reached a fiery furnace, and then, he must climb in. The friar soon reached the furnace, and there, the angel reminded him that he must climb in. Surrounding that furnace were devils with threatening pitchforks if he didn't. So he jumped in.

Once inside the furnace, the friar saw before him his old godfather. "How did you get in here?" he asked.

"Go a little farther inside and you will also see your godmother," the man replied. The friar went in farther, and he saw his godmother, also all aflame.

"Why are you undergoing such cruel torment?" he pleaded with her.

She answered him, "It happened when St. Francis foretold that famine was coming, and my husband and I lied about the measure of the grain that we sold. As a result, we're burning, here and now." The angel listened to all of this and then thrust the friar out of the furnace.

"Move on," he said. "You still have perils to experience."

"You are cruel," the friar repeated to the angel. But at that, the angel touched him once more and made him feel strong and well all over again.

Next, the angel led the friar to a narrow, slippery bridge without handrails that crossed a treacherous river. The roaring waters below were filled with scorpions and dragons, and the angel said, "Get going. You must cross."

"How can I?" the friar cried.

"Follow me, and you will," the angel replied. At this, the friar followed the angel onto the bridge and into the middle of it. But at that moment, the angel flew away and the friar remained alone on the bridge, looking down at the frightening beasts below. He was so frightened that he couldn't move. The friar cried out to Jesus for help, weeping, asking to be saved from this.

At that moment, the friar felt wings growing upon his body. He paused a few moments to wait until they were sufficient for him to fly as the angel had done. But he couldn't wait long enough and his fear overtook him; the friar tried taking to the air with his stubble wings but then fell back down, striking the bridge, clinging to it for his very life.

Again the wings seemed to grow, but slowly, and again he tried to fly, but his wings were insufficient, and he fell back onto the bridge. "If these wings begin to grow again, I will wait for them," the friar said.

Then a third time the wings grew. It seemed to the friar that 150 years went by while he waited there upon that bridge waiting for those wings to come in fully. And when they did, he was finally able to fly up to the palace where the angel had first gone. He reached the palace gate and the keeper asked of him, "Who are you and why are you here?"

"I am a Friar Minor."

"Well, wait here for a moment," the gatekeeper said, "and I will bring St. Francis to see if he recognizes you." And as the keeper went away, the friar looked around him at the beauty of the place. He saw whole choirs of angels, and saints besides. While he looked around, there appeared not only Francis, adorned with five star-like wounds of the stigmata, but also Brother Bernard, wearing a crown of stars, and Brother Giles, shining with light, and many other men and women.

"Let him come," Francis said to the gatekeeper, "for he is a friar." And he led the friar into the palace and the friar suddenly felt all sweetness and forgot all of his tribulations. Once he'd seen all of the beauties of that place, Francis said to him, "Now, my son, you have to return to the world for another seven days. While you are there, prepare yourself, and soon I will come for you again." The last thing he remembered was how disappointed he felt at having to leave the presence of those blessed ones.

Then, the friar woke up. He recovered his consciousness just at the moment that the bell was ringing for Prime.* It seemed that years had gone by during his dream, but it turned out that it was only the time from Matins until dawn.

The friar told his guardian all about his dream, and about the seven-day period that St. Francis had told him about. Then the friar came down with a fever. And seven days later, Francis came to get him with a throng of saints. To the praise and glory of God. Amen.

[#26 of 53]

---

* Prime is known as the first liturgical "hour" of daily prayer, usually beginning at 6 AM, or dawn.

CHAPTER 30

———

The source of joy, or, St. Francis and Brother Leo
walking in the freezing rain

[ca. 1221–AUGUST 1224]*

S<small>T. FRANCIS WAS OUT WALKING ONE WINTER'S DAY</small> with Brother Leo, from Perugia to St. Mary of the Angels. The air was bitterly cold.

Francis called out to Leo, who was walking a distance ahead of him, "Brother, even if the Friars Minor in every country are an example of holiness and integrity to the world, there is no real joy in that." Leo said nothing, but only kept walking.

They went on a bit farther and then Francis called out to Leo again, saying, "Brother, if a Friar Minor can help the blind to see, the paralyzed to walk, the possessed to drive out their devils, the deaf to hear, the lame to walk, the dumb to speak—even the dead to rise again after four days; you should write this down: the source of joy isn't in any of that, either."

They walked on further. Leo said nothing.

Francis called out to him yet again, saying, "Brother, if a friar knows all the languages and sciences and scriptures

———

* St. Francis and Brother Leo were frequent companions in Francis's last half-decade. Leo was even Francis's confessor. The events of this story likely happened before August 1224, because after that the narrative of Francis's life is dominated by the stigmata and his failing health.

in the world, and if he knows how to prophesy, as well as the consciences of others—write this down: there's no joy in that!"

Leo kept going. They kept walking along as they were, with Leo ahead of Francis. Francis had to call out even louder than before: "Brother! God's little sheep! If a friar can speak with the tongues of angels, and knows the courses of the stars, and the power of herbs to cure, and every treasure of knowledge in the world including about birds and fish and animals and humans and roots and stones and waters—write it down, brother: the source of joy isn't there!"

Still they kept walking and one more time Francis called out: "Brother, if a friar preaches in a way that converts all of the infidels to faith in Christ, even that is not the source of joy."

That was enough. After two miles of this, Brother Leo spun around in frustration.

"In God's name, father, please, tell me, where then is the source of joy to be found?!"

"When we arrive at St. Mary's," Francis began, "and we're soaked by the rain and chilled to the bone, completely drenched with mud and so very hungry, and we ring at the gate and the brother on duty comes to the gate and says, 'Who are you?' We will say, 'We are your brothers.' But if he argues with us and says, 'You aren't telling me the truth. I don't trust you. You might steal from us. Go away!' then he won't open the gate and we'll have to stand outside in the freezing snow and cold until night falls.

"Then, if we have to endure more insults there, and show patience and humility and charity to that brother porter—whom God has made to say what he might say, just to test us—write it down, brother: that's the source of our joy!"

Francis continued. "We may then continue to knock on the gate, and that brother will be angry now, and send us away with curses as well as blows. He might say, 'Get away from here! Who do you think you are, trying to come in here?!' If we bear all of this with patience and receive his insults with joy and charity in our hearts— write this down too, brother: that is the source of joy!

"For we bear all of this inasmuch as we bear the sufferings of Jesus Christ. We bear it all because we love him."

[#8 of 53]

CHAPTER 31

St. Francis and Brother Leo have trouble praying together

[ca. 1221–AUGUST 1224]

S T. FRANCIS WAS OUT WALKING ONE DAY WITH
Brother Leo, his closest friend and companion,
when it came time to pray the Divine Office. It was in
the earliest days of Francis's new movement, when the
brothers lived in the utmost simplicity; for this reason,
and given their remote location, Francis and Leo had
no books at hand when the hour for morning prayer
had come.

Francis said to Leo: "Since we do not have a prayer
book with us, but it is still important that we spend time
praising God, let us create something new.

"I will speak and you will answer, as I teach you.

"I will say 'O Brother Francis, you have done so many
sins and evils in this world. You are deserving of hell.'

"And you, Leo, will respond, 'So it is, Francis, you
deserve the lowest depths of hell.'"

Brother Leo nodded that he understood and gave
Francis assurances of his perfect obedience. "Let us begin,
father," he agreed.

And so Francis began the new liturgy. He said, "You
have done so many sins and evils in this world, Brother
Francis, that you are deserving of hell."

"But God will work through you so much good," Leo replied earnestly, "that surely you will go to paradise."

"No, no, no," Francis said, "that is not right. When I say my part, you must say as I have instructed you, repeating, 'You are worthy only to be set among the cursed in the depths of hell.'"

Again, in obedience, Brother Leo replied, "Willingly, father. I will do it."

This time, Francis paused and painfully considered his words. After a few moments, with tears in his eyes and while pounding his heart, Francis said in a much louder voice: "O Lord of heaven and earth, I have done so much evil and so many sins in this world that I am worthy only to be cursed by you!"

And Leo quickly replied in turn: "O Brother Francis, God will do great things for you and you will be blessed above all others!"

Francis was perplexed and more than a little bit angry.

"Why do you disobey me, Brother Leo? You are to repeat as I have instructed you!"

"God knows, father," Leo answered, "that each time I set my mind to do as you say, God then makes me say what pleases him."

How could Francis argue with this? He marveled at Leo's words, searching them for the divine purpose. Nevertheless, after some time, Francis quietly said, "I pray most lovingly that you will answer me this time as I have asked you to do." Leo agreed to try, but try as he might, again and again, he could not do as Francis wished.

Time after time, into the night, past Compline and throughout the early hours of the morning, the entreaties of Francis grew ever more passionate as Leo's joy grew ever larger. Their prayers never did match, and they never did agree, praying responsively as Francis had hoped.

[#9 of 53]

CHAPTER 32

———

Two scholars in Bologna become Franciscan friars

[c a . 1 2 2 3 – 1 2 3 2]*

ONE DAY, ST. FRANCIS ARRIVED IN THE CITY OF Bologna, and when people began to hear of his arrival, they hurried to catch a glimpse of him. Soon there was a large crowd—so large, in fact, that Francis could hardly get through it to the city square.

In the square, which was filled with men, women, and students, Francis stood up on a high spot and began to preach as the Holy Spirit told him what to say. His words were so marvelous that people thought he might be an angel. Those words were like arrows piercing the hearts of those who heard them, and Francis converted many people from sin to penitence that day.

Among those that day who were inspired by God through Francis's sermon were two highborn students that had come from the Marches of Ancona. One was named Pellegrino, from Falerone, and the other went by the name Riccieri, from Muccia. Francis knew them already, for the Holy Spirit had revealed it to him, so Francis welcomed them joyfully. "Pellegrino, you will

———

* Pellegrino's death is mentioned in this story, and he didn't die until March 1232. Riccieri died two years later, so it is likely that this story was first written down in 1233.

remain in a humble position in our order. And Riccieri, you will serve the other friars," Francis told them.

And so it was that Brother Pellegrino remained a lay brother, even though he'd already been a scholar, but he said that he didn't wish to become a priest. This humility served him well and Pellegrino grew in perfection and virtue and by God's grace in love for Jesus Christ.

So on fire was Pellegrino for Christ that he soon traveled to Jerusalem so that he could see firsthand the places where the Savior had walked. He took with him a book of the Gospels and read about the holy places as he traced where the God-man had walked, touching them with his own feet, embracing those holy steps with his arms, kissing them with his lips, and wetting them with his tears.* Pellegrino inspired devotion in anyone who watched him. Then, by God's will, he returned to Italy.

As a pilgrim for God and a citizen of heaven, Pellegrino rarely visited his wealthy family anymore. Instead he encouraged them to love God and despise the things of the world. Brother Bernard—the one who had been Father Francis's firstborn spiritual son—would say that Brother Pellegrino was one of the most ideal friars in all the world. Above all, he was a pilgrim, and he never allowed himself to find peace or comfort in creaturely or

---

* This is likely referring to the path of Christ known as the *Via Dolorosa* (Latin for "Way of Suffering") that has been established since the days of the Emperor Hadrian, tracing the steps that Jesus walked through Old Jerusalem on his way to Calvary.

temporal things. Instead he was always looking toward heavenly things and pursuing virtue and love. When he passed from this life to Christ, he was full of virtue, and miracles followed him.

Meanwhile, Brother Pellegrino's companion Brother Riccieri led an active life of service, humility, and holiness. He became a close friend of St. Francis and learned many things from him. And just as Francis had foreseen, he served the other friars, becoming minister of the province of the Marches of Ancona. There he governed with wisdom for many years, following the example of Jesus Christ, who always wanted to see action more than teaching.

On one occasion, God's will allowed a temptation to surround him. Riccieri was soon consumed with this trouble and tried to overcome it with severe spiritual disciplines and prayers and weeping all night long. He couldn't shake free from the temptation. He felt that he had been abandoned by God, since relief did not come easily. He said quietly to himself, "I will go and see Father Francis, and if he welcomes me as he usually does, then I will know that God still loves me. If he does not, I am lost."

At this time, Francis was lying ill in the bishop's residence in Assisi. There, before Riccieri came to see him, God revealed to him what was happening. Francis called for his friends, Brothers Masseo and Leo.

"Go quickly and find Brother Riccieri. Hug him and tell him that I have a special affection for him that is different from what I feel for any other friar in the world," Francis said. And obediently, Masseo and Leo did as Francis requested. Upon receiving such a loving greeting, Riccieri's soul welled up with joy, and his heart overflowed with happiness. He proceeded to the bishop's residence and found Francis there.

Despite his serious illness, Francis got up upon seeing Brother Riccieri, and hugged him. "My dear son, I have a special affection for you that is different from what I feel for any other friar in the world," Francis told him. And he made the sign of the cross on Riccieri's forehead, and then kissed him there as well. Then he said, "God gave you that temptation, but God can also take it from you." And as he said those words, the temptation dropped off that friar as though it had never meant a thing. All that was left was the complete love of God.

[#27 of 53]

CHAPTER 33

―――

St. Francis interprets a vision of Brother Leo

[1 2 2 4 – 1 2 2 6]

WHEN ST. FRANCIS WAS QUITE ILL, BROTHER LEO would take care of him with beautiful devotion. On one such occasion, when Leo was near Francis but engaged himself deeply in prayer, he became caught up in ecstasy of the Spirit and he saw a vision of a wide, teeming river.

Leo was watching people cross this river. He saw many friars go by, each carrying a load on his back. Some of the friars walked across the river one third of the way; others walked halfway; and others made it almost all the way to the other side—but then Leo watched as a strong current of water pulled all of them underwater and carried them rapidly away. All of them died a violent death in the river, crushed by the waters because they were burdened by the loads they carried on their backs into the river. Brother Leo felt deeply saddened as he saw this tragedy unfold in his vision.

But then suddenly, he saw more friars, and they had no loads to burden them. He saw that they had only poverty, and it made them shine. These friars crossed the river without any problem at all, and once Leo watched this, he woke up from his dream.

St. Francis could sense that Leo had seen a vision, and he asked him, "Describe to me what you've seen." Leo did, telling him everything.

"It was a true vision," Francis replied, "for the world is that river, and the friars who were consumed by it are the ones who no longer desire to follow the Gospel in perfect poverty. But the friars who crossed the river without harm are those who want to possess nothing of this world, nothing but Christ naked on the cross. They take the joyful burden of that cross, and that cross alone, into the world, and in obedience to Christ they pass sweetly and easily."

[#36 of 53]

———

CHAPTER 34

How St. Francis knew that Brother Elias would leave the Order

[c a . 1 2 2 5 – A P R I L 2 2 , 1 2 5 3]

S T. FRANCIS AND BROTHER ELIAS WERE STAYING together in Portiuncula when it was revealed to Francis that Elias would soon be damned, leave the Franciscan Order, and die alone. This caused Francis to pull away from the friar, to avoid speaking or eating with him, and to turn away when he saw Elias coming his way. Soon, Elias began to notice that Francis would do these things and he desired to know why. Approaching Francis one day, Francis turned aside, and Elias grabbed him to stop him from pulling away, pleading with him to say why he was avoiding him.

"It's been shown to me," Francis replied, "that you will leave our Order because of your sins and that you will die alone."

Brother Elias began to weep and threw himself on the ground at Francis's feet. "Dearest father, please, by the love of Christ, do not avoid me on account of this, but help me like a good shepherd helps his sheep!" Elias pleaded. "I beg you to pray to God on my account, so that God will remember me when I come to my end, and have mercy upon me!" Elias said this with devotion and tearfulness, and Francis was deeply moved.

So Francis prayed to God, and while he was in prayer, he was given an answer that his request had been granted and that the sentence upon Elias would be revoked in his last days. Elias wouldn't suffer damnation after all, even though he would surely leave the Order and die outside of it. That is indeed what occurred.

When King Frederick of Sicily* rebelled against the Church, the pope excommunicated him and all who were aiding him, which included Brother Elias. Elias was known then as one of the world's wisest souls, and had rebelled against both Church and his Order by going over to the other side. He too was excommunicated by the pope and stripped of his Franciscan habit.

At about that same time, Elias became very ill. When his biological brother (who was also in the Order, and remained there, in good standing) heard of Elias's sickness, he went to see him. "Brother, I am so sorry that you have been excommunicated and could die outside of the Order. Can you see a way that I might help you?" his brother asked him.

"I don't know what you could do other than go to the pope on my behalf," Elias responded. "Ask him if, for the love of Christ and of St. Francis, whom I was once

---

* When Pope Gregory IX excommunicated Emperor Frederick II (1194–1250), he called him the antichrist. Pope Innocent IV, following Gregory IX, also battled with and freshly excommunicated Frederick, calling him a heretic and a "friend of Babylon," among other things.

devoted to, to consider lifting my excommunication and restoring me to good standing."

"For your sake, I will do whatever I can for your salvation," his brother said. And leaving his side, the brother traveled to the pope and humbly asked for mercy for his brother.

So it happened that, by the assistance of the prayers of St. Francis, when his brother asked, the pope granted this request, telling the brother that if when he returned to Elias's side, Elias was still alive, he may absolve the excommunication and restore to Elias his habit.

Elias's brother hurried from the papal court back to Elias to bring him this news. When he arrived, he found Elias very near death, but still breathing, and he absolved him. Thus it was that Brother Elias put his habit back on, received the final sacrament of the Church, and died in peace.* He had placed faith in the prayers of St. Francis, and it is believed that those prayers were what brought him his final graces.

[#38 of 53]

---

* Many of the tales show marks of multiple authorship over a period of time, such as this one, which begins by declaring that Elias would die outside of the Order but then concludes by saying that his habit was restored to him.

CHAPTER 35

———

When St. Anthony preaches to the fish in the sea

[1 2 2 5 – 1 2 3 0]

O UR LORD JESUS CHRIST USED THE MOST FOOLISH
of all creatures—fish—to rebuke the world for
its foolish ignorance, just as he had once used the ass
of Balaam in the Old Testament.* In the process, Christ
showed people that they should listen to St. Anthony's
beautiful preaching and teaching.

St. Anthony was in Rimini, a place with many heretics,
desiring to show them the way back to true faith, and he
preached Christ and Holy Scripture to them for several
days in a row. But the people were hard of heart and
refused to listen. Then one day, by God's inspiration,
Anthony traveled to the mouth of the river at Rimini
and stood on the bank overlooking the sea.† He started
calling to the fish in God's name, preaching to them,
"You, fish of the waters, listen to God's word—for the
heretics refuse!" And when he said this, a huge gathering
of fish rose up before his eyes and near the bank where
he stood. They stuck their heads out of the water and
looked carefully toward Anthony. In a field of color and

———

* See Numbers chapter 22.

† Rimini is located on the eastern shore of Italy near where two major
rivers, the Marecchia and the Ausa, empty into the Adriatic Sea.

like an army readying for battle, schools of fish, large and small, situated themselves to see Anthony's face and to listen to his sermon. They were a packed crowd, looking like a horde of pilgrims heading for an indulgence, before the holy father. There, they listened with humility to what Anthony had to say.

"My fish brothers," St. Anthony said, "give thanks to God your creator, the one who gave you all that you need, whether fresh or salt water. He also gives you refuge from storms, an easy mode of travel, and the food that you need to live. When God first created you, he said, be fruitful and multiply, and he blessed you. During the Flood, as other animals died, you were saved by God completely.

"You are able to go wherever you please with your powerful fins. It was you who kept the prophet Jonah alive, and then threw him up onto dry land three days later. It was you who helped Our Lord Jesus to pay the tax when he was poor and had nothing.* It was you whom our King Jesus selected for food both before his resurrection and in a mysterious way, following it.† Because of all of this, you should praise God, who has blessed you more abundantly than other creatures."

---

* This reference is from Matthew 17:24–27. Collectors of the temple tax ask Peter why his teacher (Jesus) does not pay. Jesus instructs Peter, saying, "Go to the lake and cast a hook; take the first fish that comes up; and when you open its mouth, you will find a coin; take that and give it to them for you and me."

† For "and in a mysterious way, following it," see John 21:1–14.

Hearing all of this, the fish all nodded their heads, and some opened their mouths, praising God as best they could.

"Blessed be God! Fish in the water give God more glory than heretical people! So-called irrational creatures listen more intently to God's word than people without faith!" Anthony cried.

People began to hear of this miracle, as it was happening, and they soon came running to see. When they saw the actions of the fish, even the heretics felt sorry. They sat there and listened, too, to the words of St. Anthony, who kept on preaching. His words about the Catholic faith were beautiful that day, and by them all of the heretics came back to true belief in Christ and those who were already faithful were blessed and filled with joyfulness.

When it was all over, Anthony blessed the fish before they swam away. And when they left, they were expressing their own joy with games in the sea.

[#40 of 53]

CHAPTER 36

---

*St. Anthony of Padua preaches a sermon
that every language can understand*

[1 2 2 8 – 1 2 3 0]

ST. ANTHONY OF PADUA WAS THE CHOSEN COMPANION
of St. Francis whom Francis sometimes called his
"bishop."

On one occasion this vessel of the Holy Spirit was
preaching before the pope and his cardinals, who
represented many different lands speaking many different
tongues: Greek, Latin, French, German, Slavic, and
English. On fire with God's Holy Spirit like one of the
first apostles, Anthony preached so effectively and clearly
that every man present understood his words as if they'd
been spoken in his own language. They were all amazed.
It seemed that the original miracle of the Pentecost had
just been repeated before their eyes and ears.

"Isn't he a Spaniard?" one of them asked another.

"How can we possibly hear him in our own Greek,
Latin, French, German, Slavic, and English? We are from
so many different lands!"

Even the pope was amazed at this, as well as at
Anthony's deep knowledge of Holy Scripture. "He is the
Ark of the Covenant—a treasury of Holy Scripture!" the
pope said.

Such was the nature of those companions of St. Francis who were like soldiers with heavenly weapons, bringing sustenance with the essence of the Holy Spirit, protecting Christ's flock against traps set by the enemy.* Even the Vicar of Christ was one such as these, to the glory of our Lord, Jesus. Amen.

[#39 of 53]

---

* Another instance of multiple authors/editors: three metaphors in one sentence! In the sentence that follows, the reference is to Pope Gregory IX, a friend and follower of St. Francis. Gregory IX became supreme pontiff less than six months after St. Francis's death. He was pope from 1227 to 1241.

CHAPTER 37

The beautiful death of St. Francis and Brother Bernard

[SEPTEMBER 1226 and ca. 1242]

Brother Bernard was a man of true holiness, so much so that St. Francis praised him often. One day while Francis was devoutly at prayer, God revealed to him that Bernard was going to endure many attacks by the devil. This troubled Francis like a father who worries for his son, and Francis prayed to God for days, with many tears, asking Christ Jesus for victory over the devil in this thing.

One day, while Francis was praying fervently thus to God, God said to him, *Don't be afraid, Francis, for these temptations will not happen without my permission, and will be an exercise in virtue for Bernard. In the end, he will be victorious over them all, for Bernard is already a great one in my kingdom.*

This gave Francis great joy, and he gave thanks to Jesus for it. From that moment forward, Francis held no more reservations about the trials to come for his friend, and he held his friend in even greater esteem and love.

Francis showed this love for Bernard during his lifetime, but also on his deathbed. When Francis was dying, in the way that the patriarch Jacob had died—with his sons all around him, grieving for their departing father—he asked, "Where is my firstborn? Come to me, son, so that I may bless you before I go."

At Francis's words, Brother Bernard whispered in Brother Elias's ear (for Elias was his vicar), "Father, please go to the saint's right hand. He wants to bless you." Now, Francis had lost most of his sight by this time. Elias came close to Francis, who put his right hand on Elias's head and said, "This is not the head of my firstborn, Bernard."

Then Bernard moved to Francis's other side, to where his left hand lay. Francis crossed his arms, so as to place his right hand on the head of Bernard and his left on Elias, and said, "God the Father and our Lord Jesus Christ bless you in every way. You are the firstborn, chosen in this Order to be a holy example and to follow Jesus in Gospel poverty. Not only did you give away all that you had, but you offered yourself completely and sweetly to God. You are blessed by our Lord and by me, his poor little one. Bless your walking, your standing still, your watching, your resting, your living, and your dying.

"Anyone who blesses you will himself be blessed, and any who curse you will not go unpunished. You are now to be the head of all the brothers. Let them follow your instructions. You have the power to admit and to release any and all from the ranks. No other friar is to lord over you, and you are free to reside wherever you may wish."

Then Francis died. And after his death, the brothers revered Brother Bernard as their father. When Bernard himself was close to death, a multitude of friars came from all over the world, including the holy one, Brother Giles. When Giles beheld Bernard, he cried out with joy, "*Sursum corda*, Brother Bernard, *sursum corda!*"*

(Bernard had quietly told one of the other brothers to prepare a special place where Brother Giles might go to be in contemplation. This had been done.) Then, when Bernard came to the last hour, he raised himself up and said to his brothers, "Most dear friends, I won't say too much. But please, consider yourselves as you see me, now. This I know in my soul: not for even a thousand worlds would I have turned away from the service of our Lord Jesus Christ.

"Here and now, I confess all my sins—to Jesus my Savior, and to you. I beg you all: love each other." And after he said this, Bernard lay back in his bed and his face shown with joyfulness. The friars marveled at him again; and in that joy Bernard departed this life and left to join with the angels.

[#6 of 53]

---

* *Sursum corda* is Latin for "Lift up your hearts." Since ancient days, it has been part of the preface to the Eucharistic prayer.

CHAPTER 38

———

How St. Clare blesses bread to be broken at table with the pope*

[1228 OR 1235]

S T. CLARE WAS ST. FRANCIS'S *PIANTICELLA*, HIS "little plant," and was such a fervent follower of Christ and his cross that bishops and cardinals and even the pope wanted to see and talk with her. They all visited her, and often, in person.

On one occasion, the pope himself—knowing that Clare was a vessel of the Holy Spirit—traveled to her monastery in order to talk and listen with her about heavenly matters. They talked for a long time about salvation and praising God, and while they were talking, Clare ordered some loaves of bread. She asked that they be brought and set out on the table so that Christ's vicar might bless them.

When Clare and the pope were done talking, Clare knelt before the Holy Pontiff and asked him if he would bless the loaves. The pope said, "Faithful sister Clare, you will please bless them and make the sign of the cross over them, in honor of the one to whom you have dedicated your whole life."

"Holy Father, I cannot," she replied, "for I am a small and sinful woman who would never presume to do such a thing in the presence of Christ's own vicar."

———

* Pope Gregory IX (1227–1241).

"Don't think of it as presumption," he said, "but obedience, for I command you to bless these loaves in this way." And so, obediently, Clare devoutly made the sign of the cross over the bread, blessing them. At that moment something amazing occurred: a clearly visible cross appeared marked on the surface of each of the loaves. When the pope saw this miracle, he thanked God, and then after blessing St. Clare, he took some of the bread with him as he left.

From that moment on, St. Francis would send people with illnesses to Clare and her sisters, for it was clear that their prayers and blessings, by virtue of the cross, would restore health to God's glory. Amen.

[#33 of 53]

———

CHAPTER 39

*St. Francis appears in a vision to a friar
thinking of leaving the Order*

[1231]

A DELICATE, NOBLE YOUTH ONCE ENTERED THE ORDER
of St. Francis, and within days of taking its habit, he
began to despise it. He felt like a man wearing a sack. The
sleeves were wrong, the cowl not to his liking, and the
habit was too rough and too long. It was all unbearable to
this boy of gentle upbringing. He was quickly despising
the Order itself, thinking of returning to the world,
because of his disdain for the clothing.

His novice master at the time had taught the youth how
to kneel reverently, when passing before the altar in the
friary where the Blessed Sacrament was stored, uncovering
his head and crossing his hands upon his chest. The boy
always did this carefully. And so it was that on the very
night when the youth had decided to leave the Order,
he had to pass through the friary past the altar where the
Blessed Sacrament was stored. As before, he paused to
kneel and bow—and at that moment he was taken up in
spirit and a vision of God was revealed to him.

The boy saw before him a long line of saints, walking
in pairs, dressed in beautiful vestments, their faces and
hands shining like the sun. As they marched before his
eyes, they sang, and angels chanted, adding to the joy.

Among those marching saints were two that stood out more than all of the others; there were two that shone most brilliantly of all. The boy watched this magical procession, and when it had passed, he ran up to the saints at the end of the line and inquired, "Please, tell me who are all of these beautiful people?"

They turned to him and replied, "We are all Friars Minor in paradise."

"And who are those two who I saw shining most of all?" the boy asked.

"That was St. Francis; and with him, the last was St. Anthony, who has just died. He fought like a knight against temptation, enduring until the very end. We are all leading him in glory through paradise.

"These garments that you see us wearing were given to us by God to replace the habits that we wore on earth. And the radiance of our countenance is also God's gift to us, to replace the humility, poverty, obedience, and chastity with which we conducted ourselves in our religious lives. Keep this in mind, son," the saint said, "for if you despise the world now, you will shine in heavenly glory."

With that the vision was ended, and the youth had heard the divine words. He went away encouraged in his vocation and repented to the guardian of the friars for his prior presumptions. From that day forward, this young man accepted rough penance, and by doing so, he became a good man.

[#20 of 53]

CHAPTER 40

———

When the king of France goes in disguise to see Brother Giles

[1 2 4 0 – 1 2 6 0]

S T. LOUIS, THE KING OF FRANCE, ONCE DECIDED TO go on pilgrimage to see the shrines of the world.* Having heard of the saintliness of Brother Giles, one of the first companions of St. Francis, he decided to visit him personally in Perugia. When he arrived at the friars' gate, with only a few companions, he was dressed as a common pilgrim. He asked the porter if Brother Giles was at home, not saying who he was. So the friar went and found Giles and told him only that a simple pilgrim was looking for him.

Brother Giles knew instantly, through spiritual perception, that it was the king of France who was calling. So he bounded from his cell and ran toward the porter's gate. Once he arrived, he did not say a word but grabbed the pilgrim and hugged him, kissing him, as if the two were long-lost friends. There they remained in silence for some time. Only after a while did they leave one another, and even then, never having spoken a word.

---

* This is the only French monarch in history to be made a saint of the Roman Catholic Church: St. Louis IX (1214–70). While on the throne, he was known to wash the feet of the poor and invite the destitute to dine at his royal table. He was considered a saint throughout the Western world before he died.

St. Louis went along on his journey, and Giles returned to his cell.

Now while the king was in the process of departing, one of the friars asked one of the king's companions who that man was who had just hugged Brother Giles so lovingly. The king's companion answered that it was King Louis IX stopping on his pilgrimage. Then the companion, the king, and the others who were with them, rode away.

The friars went to Brother Giles to complain. "Brother, how could you say nothing at all to the great king who came all this way from France to see you?!" they exclaimed.

"Brothers, don't be so surprised," Giles said, "that neither of us could speak in those moments. God's light revealed who he was to me, and who I was to him, and it was by that light that we saw into each other's hearts.* We heard what we needed to hear without the movement of lips or tongues. Human voices cannot always speak of divine mysteries. Sometimes human conversation is a sad excuse for true communication."

[#34 of 53]

---

* The fame of Brother Giles is mentioned also by Salimbene of Parma (1221–ca. 1290), a thirteenth-century historian.

CHAPTER 41

———

*How St. Clare miraculously travels across
the city on Christmas Eve**

[CHRISTMAS 1252]

THERE WAS A TIME WHEN ST. CLARE WAS SO SERIOUSLY
ill at San Damiano that she was unable to get up to
say the Divine Office in church with her sister nuns. It
happened to be the Feast of the Holy Nativity of Our
Lord, and the sisters were to say Matins and then receive
Holy Communion at a Nativity Mass. Clare remained
behind in bed, sick, and sad.

But Jesus wanted his faithful spouse to be consoled, and
so he performed a miracle. In spirit, Clare was carried to
Matins and Mass at the church of St. Francis; she enjoyed
the entire celebration as done by the friars so that she
even heard the organ playing and the friars' chanting.
She received Holy Communion and was completely
consoled. Then, Jesus carried her back to her bed.

The sisters, when they had finished the Divine Office
at San Damiano, returned to see Clare. They said, "Dear
mother, Clare, what beautiful consolation this Feast of
the Nativity has been! We so wish that you could have
joined us!"

———

* In 1958, during the initial explosion of popularity of the new technology
of television, St. Clare was made its patron saint because of this legend. It
was as if she saw the whole thing on TV!

"My sisters," Clare began, "I thank God, my blessed Jesus Christ, because I was fully consoled and permitted to attend holy ceremonies this special night of all nights. In fact, the celebration that I attended was greater, even, than the one that you have just come from. By Christ, and through the intercession of St. Francis, I was there in Francis's church, hearing everything, and receiving our Lord.

"So praise God with me," she concluded, "who took me there himself. Whether I was there as you see me now, or in spirit alone, I don't know. Only God knows."

[#35 of 53]

CHAPTER 42

——

*When Brother Pacifico saw the soul of his humble
brother flying to heaven*

[1 2 3 0 – 1 2 5 0]

IN THE PROVINCE OF THE MARCHES AFTER ST. FRANCIS
had died, there were two brothers who were together
in the Order: Brother Humble and Brother Pacifico.*
They were both great in holiness.

Brother Humble lived at Soffiano,† a long way from
where Brother Pacifico lived in a community of friars. One
day, while praying, Pacifico was touched by the hand of
God and he saw his brother's soul flying directly to heaven.
Brother Humble had died.

Years later, Brother Pacifico was himself living at Soffiano,
where his brother had died, when a request came from the
house of Brunforte for the friars to leave Soffiano and move to

----

* Every translator of *The Little Flowers* makes decisions as to when to
retain the Italian, for flavor, and when to render Italian names and
words into English for sense and understanding. This is a case where
I'm using "Humble" in place of the Italian *Umile*, but retaining the
Italian original, *Pacifico*, which would be "Peace-Loving" in English.

† Raphael Brown tells us that "Soffiano was a grotto high on the steep
slopes of Monte Ragnolo, three hours' climb from Sarnano—a striking
example of early Franciscan hermitages." (Raphael Brown, ed., *The Little
Flowers of Saint Francis: First Complete Edition* [New York: Image Books,
1958], 341–42.)

another place.* The friars needed to move the remains of all of their brothers who had died in that place, and it was given to Brother Pacifico to transfer the bones of his brother, Humble. He gathered up the bones reverently and bathed them in wine, wrapped them in a white cloth, and wept and kissed them. This shocked the other friars. They looked on him as one who was putting too much care into worldly affection and showing too great a devotion to what was merely natural remains. Sensing this, Brother Pacifico explained himself.

"Dear brothers, don't be surprised," he said. "I did what I did because my brother died at a time when I was devoutly in prayer and I clearly saw his soul ascend to heaven. So I have known for certain that these are the bones of a saint and are bound eventually, also, for heavenly glory. If God had graced me with a similar knowledge about any of the other friars who were buried here, I would do likewise with their bones."

With this, the other friars understood Brother Pacifico's intentions, and all were blessed by him. They praised God from whom come all blessings wrought by his holy friars. Amen. [#46 of 53]

------

* This family of Brunforte was likely known to Brother Ugolino, the compiler of these tales. It seems that the friars were occupying the Soffiano friary only by the good graces of the lords of Brunforte. The closing of Soffiano is used by scholars today as an indication of when the original edition of the *Actus* was written—immediately afterward. They say that Soffiano closed in 1327 and these stories could then have been compiled for the first time in the year or two following that event. (See *Francis of Assisi: Early Documents*, vol. 3, ed. Regis J. Armstrong et al. [New York: New City Press, 2001], 429.)

CHAPTER 43

———

Miracles that God performed through the lives of some of the brothers

[ca. 1240 – 1290]

IN EARLIER DAYS, THE PROVINCE OF THE MARCHES OF Ancona was like a night sky filled with shining stars representing the holy and worthy friars who shone on earth and in heaven—before God and before their neighbors—in virtue. These men made the Franciscan Order and the entire world brilliant through their example and their teaching. Their memory is a blessing.

Among these there were some who were like the greatest of the constellations, shining most brightly of all. For instance, there was Brother Lucido the Elder, on fire with holiness from God. His preaching was Holy Spirit-inspired and reaped much fruit.

Another was Brother Bentivoglia of San Severino, whom Brother Masseo of San Severino once saw levitating high up in the air while out praying in the woods. It was the witness of this miracle that caused Masseo, who was then a pastor, to leave his work and become a Friar Minor. He then, too, lived a miraculous life, doing many amazing things both before and after his death. His body is buried in Muro.

But back to Brother Bentivoglia. Once when he was by himself taking care of a man afflicted with leprosy, he received instruction from his guardian to leave that place and go to another that was fifteen miles distant. Bentivoglia didn't want to leave the sick man behind, and so with love he carried him on his shoulders from dawn until sunrise the next day, going the whole fifteen miles to the new place, Monte Sancino.* Not even an eagle could have traveled that distance in such a time, and all who heard of this deed admired what he'd done as if it were a miracle.

Another saintly friar was Peter of Monticello, who was once seen by his guardian, Brother Servadeo of Urbino, floating in the air five or six yards off the ground—or, more precisely, above the floor of the church where he was praying before a crucifix. This Peter was also once overheard talking with the holy Archangel Michael on the final day of the Lent of St. Michael, which he'd been keeping most carefully and with serious devotion. This was overheard by a young friar who had hidden himself under the high altar, spying on the friar. This is what he overheard them say:

"Brother Peter, since you have worked assiduously for me and subdued your body in various ways, I will now bring you some peace. Ask me whatever you desire and I will obtain it," St. Michael said.

"Oh holy prince," Brother Peter answered him, "you defend souls in God's army. I only ask you one thing: ask God to forgive all my sins."

"Something else," the Archangel replied, "for that is already assumed."

---

* A mountain in the Marche region.

But Brother Peter could not ask anything else, and so the Archangel concluded, "Due to your great faith, I will grant your request—but also, many other things to come." And as their conversation ended (it had gone on much of that night), St. Michael the Archangel departed and Brother Peter was left alone, intensely at peace.

Another brother, Conrad of Offida, lived at the same time as Brother Peter. They were members together of the community of friars in Ancona. Once when Brother Conrad left for the woods to pray to God, Peter snuck after him in order to spy. As Conrad started to pray profoundly and with tears to the Blessed Virgin, he asked her to intercede for him before her Son so that he might feel a small measure of the delight that St. Simeon felt on the day of her purification when Simeon held the blessed Savior in his arms.* He was granted this sweet experience and more, as the Queen of Heaven appeared, together with her blessed Son, before Brother Conrad. The splendor of that dazzling Lady cleared the darkness from every corner of that place, and she placed her infant Son in Conrad's arms. Conrad took him to himself and kissed him on the lips and embraced him tightly to his heart. He felt as if his soul might melt right there and then.

Brother Peter was watching everything, and he, too, felt a sweetness in his soul. But he remained hidden in

---

* This event took place on the Feast of the Purification of the Blessed Virgin Mary, celebrated on February 2. This feast is also sometimes called Candlemas Day, or the Presentation of Jesus in the Temple. Luke 2:32 has Simeon referring to the infant Christ as "a light for revelation to the Gentiles and for glory to your people Israel."

those now-illumined woods. When the Blessed Virgin left Brother Conrad, Brother Peter snuck quickly back and was not seen. Later, as Conrad himself returned, beside himself with joyfulness, Peter called to him, "Hey, man of heaven, what love you have had today!"

"What do you mean, brother? What do you know?" Conrad replied.

"I know it well. The Blessed Virgin has come to you with her beloved Son."

But when Brother Conrad heard Brother Peter's words, he begged him to keep it quiet, for he didn't want to brag about such graces. And from that day forward, the charity between those two men was so great that it was as if they were of one heart and soul.

On one other occasion, in Sirolo,* Brother Conrad helped to liberate a young woman from the clutches of the devil by his prayers. The next morning, Conrad fled from there so that the mother of the woman couldn't find him and he wouldn't be praised by any of the crowd who knew what had happened. (Brother Conrad had prayed all the night through and had appeared before the mother in a dream while he was helping free her daughter.)

All to the praise and glory of Jesus Christ.

[#42 of 53]

---

* Another municipality in the Marches—in this case, a beautiful, ancient town that borders the Adriatic Sea.

CHAPTER 44

———

Brother Conrad shows compassion for a troublesome young friar

[ca. 1240 – 1290]

THIS BROTHER CONRAD OF OFFIDA LIVED SUCH A
saintly life of faithfulness to the Gospel, to poverty,
and to the Rule of St. Francis that our Lord Jesus honored
him with miracle after miracle while he was with us. Among
the many was the time when he was visiting the friars in
Offida and they asked him to speak with a young friar
who was acting foolishly, bothering the other members
of the community, showing little respect for the Divine
Office and the other spiritual practices of their religious
life. Brother Conrad felt great sorrow for that young man
and for the community that he was upsetting. He took
the youth aside to speak with him, and in love said many
inspiring things to show him the better way. It was as if
the hand of God came over that youth, so quickly was
he completely changed. It was as if he turned from one
man into another; the child grew quickly into a man. The
youth became obedient, thoughtful, kind, and peaceful,
eager for virtue. If the community was bothered by him
before, now they were joyful in his conversion. He was
greatly loved, as if he were almost an angel.

Now by God's will, it was very soon after this youth's
conversion that he became ill and died. The whole

community grieved, and after some days Brother Conrad, while he was praying in the friary, was greeted by the soul of the young friar. The youth's soul was coming to Conrad as a son to a father.

"Who are you?" Brother Conrad asked.

"The young friar who just died," the youth's soul replied.

"My son, how are you?" Conrad said.

"Father, by God's grace and your intercession, I am well; I was not damned. But I have to make amends for my sins and so I am suffering in purgatory. I beg you, help me by praying for me. God knows how good your prayers are!" the youth explained.

Brother Conrad agreed and first he prayed an Our Father, followed by a Requiem Mass. When he was done, the youth's soul pleaded, "Keep going, father. I am feeling so much better. Don't stop!" So Conrad went on to say one hundred Our Fathers on his behalf. And when he had finished, the youth said, "Thank you, father, for your love for me. May Our Lord give you rewards in heaven for your kindness to me because by your prayers I am now free! I am right now going to paradise!" he said, and then he was gone.

Brother Conrad told all of this—everything that had happened—to the friars there, in order to bring them joy. To the glory of Our Lord. Amen.

[#43 of 53]

CHAPTER 45

———

The Mother of Christ and John the Evangelist appear to Brother Peter

[c a . 1 2 4 0 – 1 2 9 0]

T HERE WAS ONCE A TIME WHEN THIS SAME BROTHER
Conrad and Brother Peter,* two of the brightest stars
in the holy firmament of the Province of the Marches,
were living simultaneously at Ancona. They loved each
other, and were so much of the same heart and mind that
they agreed they would always reveal to one another
whatever graces God granted to them.

Once, after they had made this agreement, Brother
Peter found himself devoutly meditating on Christ's
passion. The Blessed Mother and John the beloved
disciple together with Blessed Francis with his stigmata
were all standing there as well. Peter suddenly wondered,
with a holy curiosity, which of those three beloved ones
had endured the most because of Christ's passion. Was it
the mother who birthed him, or the much-loved one who
rested on his breast, or St. Francis who was also "crucified"?
While Peter was considering this, the Virgin appeared
before him with St. John and St. Francis—they were all
dressed in heavenly garments—and Francis's appeared
more beautiful even than John's. Peter was afraid of what

———

* This is the same Brother Peter of Monticello who appeared for the first
time two stories earlier.

he saw. But it was St. John himself who reached out to him and said, "Brother, don't be scared, and don't doubt, but know for sure that Christ's Mother and I grieved more than any others over Christ's passion, but after our time it was St. Francis who felt the greatest sorrow. For that reason, you are seeing him so gloriously."

"But most holy apostle, why does Francis's clothing seem brighter than even yours?" Peter asked of John.

"Because he wore simpler clothes than I did while he was here," St. John replied. And he reached out and gave Peter a garment that he was holding in his hand. "Take this," he said, "for I brought it to show to you." And John wanted to put it on him.

But at that moment, Brother Peter woke up from his vision. He began to shout, running to Brother Conrad. "Quickly, quickly! See what's happening, here, for it is incredible!" he shouted to him. But the vision was gone. Nevertheless, Brother Peter told Brother Conrad all that had happened.

[#44 of 53]

CHAPTER 46

The holy life of Brother John of Penna

[c a .   1 2 4 0 – 1 2 9 0]

Brother John of Penna* was also one of the brightest stars in the firmament of the province of the Marches. While he was still a boy living in the world, another, more beautiful lad appeared before him and said, "Go to Santo Stefano, John, where a friar of mine is going to be preaching. Believe all that he has to say. Listen carefully, and afterward you will have a journey before you. Eventually, you will come to me."

John did as he was told and felt a change in his soul before he had even left for Santo Stefano.† But then when he arrived, he saw many men and many women already there, from villages all over, anxious to hear the word of God. The friar-preacher was Brother Philip, one of the first friars who ever came to the Marches of Ancona. Brother Philip got up and began to preach with great fervor, not with great learning, but by simply telling about God's kingdom, the Spirit of Christ, and the path of eternal life. When the sermon ended, the boy (who later became Brother John) went up to Brother Philip and

---

* Penna San Giovanni, a hill-town in the Marches south of Ancona.

† There are more than twenty municipalities in Italy with this name, plus two islands, so it is unclear which one is intended here.

asked, "If you would have me in your Order, I would do penance and serve our Lord."

Philip knew holy innocence when he saw and heard it, as well as readiness to serve the Lord, and so he said to the boy, "Come and visit me in Recanati some day in the future, and I will receive you there." (A chapter of that province was going to be held in Recanati.)

"Surely this will be that long journey that was told to me, the one that I have to make before I may go to heaven," the boy thought to himself, with the innocence that only a youth might have. He was imagining that heaven would come as soon as he was received as a friar. And so he went. And so he was somewhat disappointed.

During that provincial chapter, the minister spoke these words: "If there are any here who desire to go to the province of Provence,* I will send them." When Brother John heard this, he wanted to go, thinking that perhaps finally this would be that journey he was to make before going to heaven. But he was shy and kept quiet.

Finally, he whispered to Brother Philip, "Father, can you please ask for me, so that I can go to Provence?" (In those days a friar would offer to travel long distances to unfamiliar places in order to become a true pilgrim and stranger in the world.) Brother Philip asked permission

* This was truly a long journey, from the Marches region of Italy to the French Riviera.

on John's behalf, and John set out joyfully, certain that he was about to finish the long-anticipated journey to heaven.

But in reality, John stayed in Provence twenty-five years, living all the while with this sort of simplicity and simple sanctity, hoping each day would be the one where the promise might be fulfilled in his life. He grew holier and more virtuous and was greatly loved by all in that place, even though he could never quite see where and when his desires might be granted to him.

Until one day when he was praying and crying out loudly to God, complaining that his earthly pilgrimage was taking too long, the blessed Lord Jesus appeared in front of him. Brother John's soul fell to pieces at that moment, and Christ said, "Son, Brother John, you may ask me whatever you desire."

"I cannot speak, my Lord," he stammered. "I don't want a thing from you but one: for you to forgive my sins. And then, allow me to see you again like this when I need forgiving again."

"Your prayer is granted," Jesus said, and then he vanished. Brother John couldn't see him anymore, but he felt completely comforted.

When at long last the friars from the Marches got wind of Brother John's holy reputation, they asked the minister-general that a note be sent to John sending him back to the Marches. When that note arrived, John was delighted to go, and said, "This is surely the long journey that was promised to me, by which I shall go to God." But when he arrived in his home province, no one even recognized him, not even his closest family. Still, he waited with patience for God's mercy in fulfilling that old promise.

Still, he lived longer. For thirty more years he stayed in the Marches and eventually served even as guardian there. Many miracles were performed through his life.

Among his gifts was the spirit of prophecy, as on one occasion when he was away and one of his novices was grabbed by the devil and tempted to leave the Order. That novice yielded but said only that he would wait to leave until Brother John returned. While he was away, Brother John's gift of prophecy told him of both the temptation and the resolution of that novice. "Come with me," John said to him, upon his return. "I want to hear your confession."

The boy sat down. Then, Brother John began, "First of all, listen to me," he said. And he told the novice all that God had shown him. Then he finished by saying, "But because you waited for me and didn't leave without receiving my blessing, God has shown his grace to you, in that you will never leave this Order. You will die as a Friar Minor with God's blessing." With that, the novice was made strong and indeed, he persevered and became a friar.

It was Brother John himself who told me, Brother Ugolino, these things.

He was also a man with great peace of mind. He did not often speak, but was a person of quiet and prayer. After Matins he would never return to his cell, but would stay bowed in the church throughout the night until dawn. One night while he was praying in this way, an angel of God came and said to him, "Brother John, your journey is soon coming to an end. What you have desired is coming true. Now you have a decision to make. Which grace do you choose: one full day in purgatory, or seven days of suffering here on earth?"

Brother John chose seven days of suffering here. He immediately then felt sick. He had a fever and many pains. He had gout in his hands and feet. And he had gastrointestinal troubles, suffering greatly from it all. But worse than all of that was a devil that stood in front of him with a large scroll and read all of John's sins and failings. "These are the reasons why you are going to hell!" the devil said to him. And our ill friar believed him—so much so, that when someone asked him how he was feeling, he said, "Awful! I am damned!"

The oldest friars of the Marches saw what was happening and they sent for Brother Matthew of Monterubbiano, one of Brother John's oldest friends. Matthew came to see him. "How are you doing?" he said, greeting his friend.

"Awful! I am damned!" was Brother John's reply.

"Impossible," Matthew said. "Do you remember confessing your sins? I was your priest and I absolved you completely.

"Also, remember your life. You have served God faithfully. God's mercy is greater than all of the sins in this world, and Jesus paid the price to redeem us of our sins. You can be completely sure of your salvation," Brother Matthew concluded.

Brother John was comforted by this, and also, his seven days of sickness were expiring and so the temptations flew away. "You must be tired," he said to Matthew. "Go lie down and rest." Matthew didn't want to go but John insisted, and so finally, Matthew lay down. Brother John then remained alone, except for the one friar who remained to care for him. While they were there, Jesus Christ came in a brilliant light, wrapped in a sweet fragrance, just as he promised that he would, when John would need him again. It was Jesus who cured John completely that time.

Then Brother John folded his hands and prayed to God with thanks for the long journey that his life had taken, and for the joyful end that was coming. He gave his soul up to God and passed from this life into the next.

His body is buried in Penna San Giovanni. To Christ's glory. Amen.

[#45 of 53]

CHAPTER 47

———

How the Blessed Mother appeared to one of the brothers

[ca. 1240 – 1290]

IN THOSE SAME MARCHES OF ANCONA, IN THAT SAME lonely place called Soffiano, there was a Friar Minor whose name I cannot recall, but he was so holy that he seemed almost like a god. He was often caught up in the direct experience of our Lord.

On one of these occasions, while his mind was ecstatically wrapped up in God, a flock of birds came and rested upon his head, his shoulders, his arms, and his hands. They just sat there and began to sing melodiously. When he emerged from his contemplation, his face showed forth a joy that seemed angelic, wholly in communion with the divine. It surprised everyone who looked upon him.

This friar was always off alone and spoke on rare occasions. He prayed all the time. Whenever someone asked him a question, he answered with more the quietude of an angel than the bluster of a man. He was always reverent and kind and his words, always divine.

He lived this way, practicing virtues, until his angelic life came to an end. He became sick and could no longer keep food down. He rejected medicine for his sick body, placing all of his faith in Christ his heavenly physician, and in his Blessed Mother. In fact, the Virgin visited and comforted him in many ways in those last days. Once, while he was alone in bed and contemplating his death, the Blessed Mother came to him with a group of angels and holy virgins amid a bright light; she approached him, very close to his bed, and when he glimpsed her, his mind and body were filled with joy.

The friar begged her to pray to her Son that he might leave the prison of the flesh.

"Don't fear, my son," she told him, "your prayer is being granted. Besides, I have seen your tears and have come to bring you a little comfort in your last earth-bound days." Then she revealed the three virgins who had accompanied her, and the electuary boxes that they were carrying.* These were so full of sweetness that the house was filled with their fragrance as the Blessed Virgin opened each one.

With a spoon in her lovely hand, she dipped it into the first box and offered some of the electuary to that sick brother. He tasted it and its sweetness fed his soul and made him want to leave his body behind. "No more, dear Lady, holy physician," he said, "I can't take any more sweetness!" But the Mother of God fed him more, until that first box was completely empty, and she talked with him about her Son, Jesus.

---

* An *electuary* is just what the story says: a medicinal paste or powder with added sweeteners (usually natural ones, such as syrup or honey), added to help make the taking of one's medicine more pleasant. Today this word is most common in veterinary medicine.

Then, she took the next box and, as she placed the spoon in it, the sick friar said to her, "Blessed Mother of God, I can't take it. My soul will melt away completely!"

"My son," she responded, "you need a little bit from this box." And after a small amount, she said to him, "That's enough. Now, be happy, because I am coming back soon to lead you to my Son and the kingdom that you have desired." Then she said goodbye to the friar, and she was gone. He remained where he was, but completely at peace. The pharmacist of heaven had given him medicine by the hand of the Blessed Virgin.

For his remaining days, the friar took no food, even though he felt strong from the divine medicine that prepared him for heaven. His spiritual vision was enhanced and he could even see the book of eternal life on which were written the names of all who would be saved from final judgment. Only a few days later, he passed from this unhappy place to the Lord Jesus. He was talking with the other friars with joy when it finally happened. To Christ's glory. Amen.[*]

[#47 of 53]

---

[*] It is interesting that this unique tale does not even include the most basic of details—the friar's name. Perhaps there was a disagreement on that point, or Ugolino is making the point that it doesn't really matter.

CHAPTER 48

———

When God showed Brother James of Massa true secrets

[1247 – ca. 1274]

BROTHER JAMES OF MASSA WAS A MAN WHO KNEW God's secrets because God showed them to him, giving James a perfect understanding of Scripture and all things to come. He was saintly to the point that Brother Giles of Assisi and Brother Mark of Montino knew of no one on earth who would be greater in the sight of God. Brother Juniper and Brother Lucido agreed.

Now while Brother John (the companion of Brother Giles) was my spiritual director, I wanted to see this Brother James. My desire was prompted by a comment of Brother John. He said to me, "If you want an understanding of the spiritual life, you must talk with Brother James of Massa. Even Brother Giles wanted his instruction. Brother James has all the secrets of heaven. All of his words are those of the Holy Spirit."

There was one time when Brother James was so caught up in God that it progressed to the point where he lay unconscious for three days—so long that the other friars began to wonder if he might be dead.* While

---

* Readers may have noticed that this theme is repeated several times in the *Fioretti*. Interestingly, St. Francis didn't advocate this sort of prayer as a virtue in itself. See the earlier "Why Brother Rufino has to preach in Assisi in his underwear" (chapter 10).

he rapturously lay there, God gave to him a deep understanding of both Scripture and the future. I heard about this, and my desire to consult with him then grew greater. When that opportunity finally came, by God's grace, I asked Brother James, "Is it true what I have heard, that God gave you knowledge of the future, including the future of our Order? Brother Matthew, whom you told under obedience, said as much." (Brother Matthew was the minister of our province of the Marches, and had forced Brother James to tell him what happened during that three-day rapturous period. Matthew would often say to the other friars: "I know one of you whom God has shown the future and many unimaginable secrets.")*

Now, this is what Brother James told me. This is what God showed to him: There was a tall and beautiful tree with roots made of gold and fruits in its branches that were made of men. Each of the branches of the tree was a province in our Order, and there was a fruit on each branch for each Friar Minor of that province. He could see there on that tree every member of our Order, including his face and age and virtues and sins.

He saw Brother John of Parma standing tallest in the tree, on the center branch, and near him at the top of the branches closest to the center branch were the ministers of every province. Atop it all was Christ sitting on a

---

* By our standards, this would be quite a breach of confidence, but it seems acceptable in the milieu of the early Franciscans!

large, white throne, speaking with St. Francis and giving him a drink from a chalice filled with life.

"Go visit all of your brothers," Christ said to St. Francis, "for the devil will always attack them and many will fall away." Two angels were given to Francis to accompany him.

After this, St. Francis came down and began to offer the chalice to each of the friars. He started with Brother John, the minister-general, who drank from it quickly and then, as a result, began to glow like the sun. Then Francis offered that chalice with the spirit of life to each of the other friars, one by one, and it became clear that most of them did not drink from it with much reverence or enthusiasm. Those who did glowed as well. And those who did not drink devoutly, or spilled some, began to look dark and deformed and devilish.

More than any of the friars on the tree, Brother John drank most fully and shone most brightly. He seemed to then sense that a storm was coming straight toward that tree, a tempest that would batter those branches, and so he traveled from the top to the bottom and hid himself away in the most solid part of the tree trunk. There, he prayed.

Meanwhile, Brother Bonaventure, who had drunk from the chalice and spilled some of it,* ascended up the tree

---

* This apocalyptic vision reveals the conflicts going on in the Order between the Spirituals and the Conventuals. Bonaventure (1221–74) was the minister-general of the Franciscan Order from 1257 (elected at the young age of thirty-six) until his death, which may have been by poisoning. He was canonized, but not until 1482—long after *The Little Flowers* was written down.

and took the spot that Brother John had left. And while Bonaventure was there, his fingernails were sharpened like iron razor blades, and he suddenly seemed to want to attack Brother John. Brother John could see this, and cried out to Christ on his throne to help. Hearing his cries, Christ summoned St. Francis, giving him a stone of flint and telling Francis, "Go cut the nails of Brother Bonaventure, for he wants to tear down Brother John!"

St. Francis did as Christ had ordered, and Brother John remained where he was, shining.

Then, a hurricane rose up and hit that tree so strongly that all of the friars began to fall off the branches. Those who had spilled from the chalice were the first to fall, and as they fell, they were carried away by devils. But as the other friars—the ones who had drunk devoutly—fell, they were carried away by angels toward the light of heaven.

He saw all of this clearly in his vision, and remembered carefully all of the details. The hurricane lasted, by God's will, until all the tree was torn up from the roots and scattered into the ground. But when the storm stopped, those golden roots showed forth out of the ground, and a new tree that was golden and full of fruit and flowers grew up beautifully in its place.

I am not omitting anything from my retelling of this vision, for every detail seemed important to me. Brother James remarked that our Order would be reformed in a different way from how it was originally founded.

Without a clear leader, the Holy Spirit will use the uneducated, the simple, the plain, and those who are despised by others in order to bring Christ's love again into the world. Christ has increased the number of these in many places, and now they only need a good shepherd who is modeled after their Shepherd, Christ.

[#48 of 53]

CHAPTER 49

——

Christ appears to Brother John of La Verna

[1275 – 1322]

THE HOLY SPIRIT MADE SO MANY BEAUTIFUL FOLLOWERS of St. Francis in his Order that we can see the truth of what Solomon said, that the beauty of a father is seen in his sons.* Standing among all of these is one other special one, the holy Brother John of Fermo, who stands out like a brilliant star in the night sky. Brother John spent so much time associated with the holy place of La Verna, even dying there, that he is also called Brother John of La Verna.

When he was but a boy, his heart was like that of a wise old man. He desired even then a life of penance and began to wear a breastplate of iron mail and a band on his flesh. By these, he was carrying a cross of self-denial throughout the day. Especially while he lived in Fermo, among the canons who were more spiritually lax in their practices, he would strictly avoid all manner of physical comfort and deny his body with joy. But those companions of his took his breastplate from him and were offended by his zealous abstinence. In many other ways they hindered him, until he determined to leave the

---

* Perhaps Proverbs 17:6, "Grandchildren are the crown of the aged, and the glory of children is their parents."

world behind and offer his holy desires to the Order of St. Francis, founded by the one of whom he'd heard saw the wounds of the crucifixion replicated in his body.

He received the habit of a Friar Minor while still a youth, and was committed for spiritual instruction to a novice master. His fervor would roast like fire when he heard that master speak of God, and inside he felt that his young heart would melt like wax in that heat. He would become so stirred up by the sensation of God's love in his heart that he would jump up and run around the garden or woods or church, as God's spirit moved him. Eventually, as he grew older, his mind was strengthened and his virtue increased, and those ecstatic feelings became like the joyful expressions of an angel in high heaven. At special times, he felt the holy embrace and kiss of Christ and his love, both in his soul and exteriorly, too.

So it happened one day, while on Mt. La Verna, that Brother John's heart was on fire with the love of God in one of these extraordinary ways, and it then lasted constantly for three years. But in God's way of caring for his most special sons, sometimes to keep them humble or to fire their desire for holiness, God decided to take from Brother John that spiritual fire, leaving him lonely and depressed. Suddenly, his soul no longer felt that beloved presence.

Grieving, he ran through the woods, calling out and crying as if for a friend who had left him behind, and without whom he would never again have any peace. He couldn't and didn't find Christ anywhere, and he definitely did not feel any of those holy embraces. He underwent this trial for many days on end until at last—when God knew that he had been tested enough—one day Brother John was sitting in the woods alone, tired and sad, leaning against a beech tree. And as he lifted his face up to heaven with tears running down his cheeks, our Lord stood right there on the path behind him, speaking not at all. When John saw him, he threw himself down at his feet and wept, begging him: "Without you, my Lord, my Savior, there is only darkness and sadness. With you, I have everything: redemption, love, desire. Be my light once again, my loving shepherd. I am your lamb."

But sometimes a man grows in love and virtue even more if and when God does not come easily—and this time, Christ went away, leaving him on the path.

Brother John saw him going, without even answering what he had said. So John jumped up and ran after Christ. Catching up to him, he again threw himself at Christ's feet, holding them fervently, and in tears, saying, "Sweet Jesus, pity me! I am suffering! Please grant my prayer, for the sake of my dark soul," he exclaimed.

But again, the Savior left him on the path, without saying a word. In fact, this time it seemed that Christ was going to leave completely. In reality, Christ was in those moments like a mother breastfeeding her baby, when she takes her breast away for a moment in order to make the child take it more eagerly when it returns.

So Brother John ran after Christ for a third time, crying like that baby seeking its mother. When John reached the spot where he was, Christ turned and looked upon him with such joy and love, holding out arms of mercy, that John saw only light coming from Christ's body. The entire forest around them was lit up with divine luminosity. Then, at that precise moment, the Holy Spirit revealed to John what he should do next: and he threw himself down at the feet of the Savior. There, John wept like a new Magdalene* and said, "I beg you, Lord, reawaken my soul!"

While Brother John was praying, he began to receive the renewal of God's grace and peace—so much that he indeed felt like Mary Magdalene. He felt that fire of God's love and presence returning to him and he gave thanks to God, kissing Christ's feet. Then John lifted up his head to look into the Savior's face. Christ held out his hands, and John kissed them. Leaning even closer, now, he hugged Jesus tightly and kissed his holy breast.

Before long, this rapturous experience of Brother John's was about to be over. The Blessed One disappeared before his eyes, but yet the deep consolation and divine knowledge remained with him. It is not so much that he

---

* A reference to the story told in Luke 7:36–50, when a sinful woman, likely a prostitute, anoints Jesus' feet while he is dining with some Pharisees. Medieval theologians identified this woman as Mary Magdalene, one of Jesus' earliest followers, but most scholars today believe that the woman from Luke 7 is actually someone else.

discovered the human Christ in those special moments, but he discovered his own soul deep within the divine Christ. (It was the one who heard about all of this from Brother John that then told it to me.)

This would be demonstrated in many clear ways to come. For example, Brother John would speak in such luminous words before the curia in Rome and before master theologians and doctors of canon law that it was inexplicable to them where he had gotten such inspiration. John was an uneducated man speaking of the most subtle matters of divine understanding, including the meaning of the Holy Trinity and other matters deeply mysterious in our Scriptures.

If you would like to further understand how Brother John came first to Christ's feet in tears, and then to his hands, and last to his holy breast, read St. Bernard on the Song of Songs. And giving these graces to Brother John without speaking a word shows us what the Good Shepherd does and how God's kingdom is not in external sounds and things but in the inner depths of the heart. As the psalmist says, glory to God comes from within.*

[#49 of 53]

---

* This could refer to many passages, for example, Psalm 84:1–3: "How lovely is your dwelling place, O LORD of hosts! My soul longs, indeed it faints for the courts of the LORD; my heart and my flesh sing for joy to the living God."

CHAPTER 50

*Brother John of La Verna's saying of Mass frees
many souls from purgatory*

[1 3 0 0 – 1 3 2 2]

THERE WAS ONCE AN ALL SAINTS' DAY WHEN Brother John of La Verna was saying Mass for the souls of the dead—who know that nothing is better for them than the Holy Sacrament. Brother John's words were so full of love and compassion that day that his devotion seemed to be completely otherworldly.

When he came to elevate the holy Body of Christ, offering it to God the Father, he suddenly saw innumerable souls rushing out of purgatory like sparks blasting out of a blazing furnace. He saw these human souls fly to heaven by the merits of Christ, who suffered on the cross for the salvation of all humankind. This is the sacrifice that is offered up each day in the most holy Body—for both living and dead. That One is the blessed God-man, light and life, redeemer and judge, who is our Savior now and forever. Amen.

[#50 of 53]

CHAPTER 51

————

The tale of Brother James and Brother John

[1 3 0 0 – 1 3 2 2]

THERE WAS ALSO A TIME WHEN BROTHER JOHN OF La Verna heard about a serious illness of the holy Brother James of Fallerone, who was staying in the friary at Mogliano. From the friary at Massa, John began to pray with all of his heart for James's recovery—that it would be God's will for him to recover, for Brother John loved Brother James as a father loves a son.

While he was praying, Brother John became so caught up in God that he began to see angels and saints in the sky above his head. There, in the woods, he saw them shining brightly, illuminating everything. Among the angels, John saw Brother James, ill, but standing among them in radiant, white clothes. He also saw the blessed Father Francis, with his holy stigmata, also shining in glory. And there were Brother Lucido and Brother Matthew the Elder, too, and other friars whom Brother John had never known in this earthly life, together with the saints, all of them shining above his head.

John just stood there and gazed on them all with delight. And the vision revealed to him that James would indeed die from this illness, but that his soul would be saved. James would not go to heaven right away, but that soul of his would need to be purified in purgatory first.

After seeing all of this, John was full of joy for the salvation of his brother friar—so much so that he didn't even grieve over his impending death. From that moment forward, he began to think of James in these terms, "My dear brother, Christ's faithful servant, God's friend, companion of the angels and saints!"

Soon after this vision, Brother John left the friary at Massa and traveled to the friary at Mogliano, where he found Brother James so weak from illness that he could no longer speak. John told James that by a revelation he knew that he would die, but also that his soul would be saved. This filled James with joy. You could see the joy on his face, for he began to smile, with happy expressions thanking his brother for such wonderful news.

Then, Brother John asked Brother James if he would return to him, after he died, to tell him how it was. James promised that he would, if Christ allowed it. Then, as he died, he began to speak with the words of the psalmist and said, "Ah, in peace . . . Ah, in him . . . Ah, I go to sleep . . . Ah, I now rest!"* Thus, he died, leaving this life to go to Christ. His body was then buried and John returned to

---

* See Psalm 3:5, "I lie down and sleep; I wake again, for the LORD sustains me." And Psalm 4:8, "I will both lie down and sleep in peace; for you alone, O LORD, make me lie down in safety." *Death* is often called *sleep* in the Bible.

the friary in Massa, where he waited for James to come to him someday, as he said he would try to do.

One day, while he was praying, Christ showed himself to Brother John. There were angels and saints all around Christ, but not James, and so John began to quickly praise his brother to Christ.

On the following day, while John was again praying, James came and appeared before John. James was surrounded by angels. John said, "Holy father, you didn't come right away to tell me how it was, as you said that you would!"

"I needed to be purified first," Brother James replied. "It was during the same hour that Christ appeared before you that I showed myself to Brother James of Massa while he was serving at Mass. He saw the host changed into the beautiful face of a boy, and I said to him, 'I am going to God's kingdom today with him, for no one can go there without him!' That was also at the same moment when you were praising me before Christ. Your prayers were heard and I was set free," Brother James concluded.

At this, Brother James of Fallerone returned to the Lord and Brother John was overjoyed. This same Brother James died on the Feast of St. James the Apostle in July and was buried at the friary of Mogliano. To this day, he performs miracles.

[#51 of 53]

CHAPTER 52

———

When Brother John of La Verna saw how every created thing relates to its Creator

[1300 – 1322]

Now Brother John of La Verna's holiness was such that he would often receive special revelations upon the greatest feast days of our blessed Lord Jesus Christ. So it happened once as the Feast of the Nativity was approaching that the Holy Spirit gave to him an intense and burning love for Christ. Brother John suddenly glimpsed the love by which the Savior had humbled himself to take on our humanity—so much so that he was frightened to death and felt that he might faint. His heart began to burn intensely to the point where it felt as hot as a furnace inside him. He couldn't help himself: he shouted out loud.

Now at that very moment when he felt this incredible divine love, a powerful surety of salvation flooded over him and he felt that, if he were to die there and then, he wouldn't even need to make his way through purgatory. This supreme love lasted for a half year without any interruptions. The intensity of feeling the love lasted even longer, for more than a year. It took hold of him so much, at times, that Brother John felt he might actually be dying. Even when this time came to an end, he still received many loving kindnesses from God, and countless revelations. I myself observed these with my own eyes on several occasions, as did others.

Among these, there was one night in particular when Brother John was raised to such a level of knowing God that he was able to see the image of the Creator in all created things, in heaven and on earth, each in its own way, including how the choirs of angels are arrayed under God and how the paradise of earth and our blessed humanity are under Christ. He also saw lower realms, and understood how every created thing relates to its Creator and how God is above, within, around, and outside of all of them.

After this God raised him up, above all other creatures, and his soul was completely absorbed in the light of God, and settled deeply into the ocean of God's infinitudes.* Brother John, at this point, was unable to feel or see or think or speak of any of those things that the human heart usually can feel or see, think or speak of. He was so caught up in the divine that it was as if his soul was completely absorbed in the ocean of God. A drop in the sea knows not itself, but only the sea.

---

* This image of a drop in the ocean, for the experience of salvation/ liberation, isn't found in any of the earliest writings of the Franciscan movement. But curiously, it is present in the mystical writings of many religious traditions throughout the world. Compare to the principle of *moksha* in Hinduism, the stories of the Hasidic masters in Judaism, and the poems of Rumi in Sufism. However, at the end of this paragraph, the author makes it clear that Brother John's experience was thoroughly Trinitarian.

Even so, Brother John's soul knew this God-sea as three Persons in One.

He could feel the love that caused the Son of God to become man in obedience to the will of his Father, and he meditated on the Incarnation and passion of the Son. Brother John said that there is no way for the soul to be contained in God, or to find everlasting peace, but through the Son, Christ, the way, the truth, and the life.* Everything was shown to him, then, including what Christ did from the time of the very fall of the first man until the God-man ascended into heaven. It is this Christ who is the leader of all of his chosen ones since the beginning of the world until the end of time. Amen.

[#52 of 53]

---

* Cf. John 14:6. This entire story is full of the mystical imagery in John's Gospel.

CHAPTER 53

———

When Brother John of La Verna fell down while saying Mass

[1 3 0 0 – 1 3 2 2]

SOMETHING INCREDIBLE ONCE HAPPENED TO THAT same Brother John. Some of the friars who were there have told me all about it. This occurred once while he was staying in the friary of Mogliano in the Marches.

It happened during the first night after the eight-day Feast of St. Lawrence (within the eight-day Feast of the Assumption of the Blessed Virgin Mary), when John woke up early before Matins. At the Matins service, as he recited the prayers with the others, the Lord filled his soul with supremely good things. And when Matins was over, he went walking through the garden, filled with God's grace and sweetness, so much so that he began to shout out those words of our Lord, *"Hoc est Corpus Meum!"* "This is my body!" The Holy Spirit had enlightened him through those words.

Brother John's soul could see with clarity Jesus Christ and the Blessed Virgin and all the angels and saints. He clearly understood the words of the apostle that we are all one in the body of Christ, each of us is one with the other, and with the saints we may see and understand the inclusive dimensions and depth of Christ's love.* This love is greater than all knowledge, and we may know it when those words, *Hoc est Corpus Meum*, bring the Holy Sacrament before us.

By dawn, Brother John walked into the church in this passion and fervor brought on by divine grace. He couldn't help himself but shouted it out three times. He thought that no one was there or would hear him, but there was one friar praying alone in the choir and he heard.

Brother John remained like this until the time came when he was to celebrate Mass. When he put on his vestments and moved toward the altar, the passion of his devotion and Christ's affection swelled within him to the point where he had an overwhelming sense of God's ineffable presence. He was suddenly afraid that these feelings might lead to him interrupting the Mass and so he paused to consider what to do next. Then he recalled that something like this had happened to him once before, and all had gone well, so he thought that he could proceed this time, too. But he was still wary, for the divine can easily interrupt the human.

---

* These are both passages from the Apostle Paul: "For as in one body we have many members, and not all the members have the same function, so we, who are many, are one body in Christ, and individually we are members one of another" (Rom. 12:4–5). And, "I pray that you may have the power to comprehend, with all the saints, what is the breadth and length and height and depth, and to know the love of Christ that surpasses knowledge, so that you may be filled with all the fullness of God" (Eph. 3:18–19).

He got as far in the Mass as the Preface of the Blessed Virgin. Everything was fine, but then the divine sweetness began to overcome him. When he came to the *Qui pridie,** he felt completely overwhelmed. He came to the consecration itself and began to say those words over the host, repeating *Hoc est . . . Hoc est . . .* again and again, unable to continue. He couldn't say the words, for he believed that he saw Christ before his eyes, together with angels and saints. He felt as if he were going to faint.

At this, the guardian of the friary came running to help. He stood beside Brother John, as did another friar with a lit candle. Meanwhile, other friars, and men and women, and many of the most prominent people of the province who were there to hear Mass, stood concernedly around the altar. Some of them were crying, as women are prone to do.†

Brother John was just standing there, consumed with joy and happiness. He'd paused during the words of consecration, but only because he could see that Christ was not entering the host—or, instead, that the host was not changing into the Body of Christ—because he hadn't yet spoken the second half of the formula . . . *Corpus Meum.*

---

* This is the beginning of the paragraph during the Mass leading up to the *Hoc est Corpus Meum,* when the priest says "*Qui pridie quam pateretur, accepit panem . . .*" or "Who, the day before he suffered, took bread. . . ." In other words, Brother John was coming to that portion of the Mass that had previously so profoundly moved him.

† Such a statement would have been common 100 years ago, let alone 700 years ago, when this was written down.

And so, after what seemed a very long time, unable to bear the majestic, mystical revelation of these things, he loudly exclaimed, ". . . *Corpus Meum!*" Immediately, bread vanished from sight and the host showed only the Lord Jesus Christ. At this, Brother John's humility and adoration left him unable to continue speaking the remaining words of the consecration. He fell backward and was caught by his guardian who was still standing next to him. The others in the church rushed forward, and they all carried John into the sacristy and laid him down. His body had quickly gone cold. He seemed to be dead. His fingers were stiff and bent so that they couldn't be opened or even budged. He laid there as if dead until the time of Tierce.*

Now, I was among those present that day, and I wanted to know what had truly happened to him. So as soon as he came to, I went and asked him all about it. He used to confide often in me, and by God's grace he told me everything. He told me that both before and after the words of consecration, his heart became inside of him like hot wax, and his body seemed boneless, to the point where he couldn't lift either his arms or hands to make the sign of the cross over the host. Before he ever became a priest, he said, God told him that he would faint like that during Mass. He had said many Masses without it happening and had begun to wonder if the

---

* Probably about two and a half hours later.

prophecy was not from God. Then, fifty days before this day—before the Assumption of the Blessed Virgin, when all of this happened—it was again revealed to him that it would happen, but he'd forgotten.

[#53 of 53]

BRIEF BIOGRAPHICAL SKETCHES
OF THE FRIARS

The first three to join Francis . . .

BROTHER BERNARD OF QUINTAVALLE remained a lay brother (not a priest), as did all but one of the first twelve followers of St. Francis. Like many of the earliest followers, Bernard came from a prominent and wealthy family in Assisi. He was the first to become a full-time companion of Francis. This happened in April 1209, and on April 16, 1209, Francis, Bernard, and Peter Catani opened the Scriptures together. Bernard later recruited the first friars in Bologna, in 1211. He died in the early 1240s in Assisi.

BROTHER PETER CATANI joined St. Francis and Bernard to open the Gospels together at the home of the bishop of Assisi on April 16, 1209. They read Matthew 19:21, Luke 9:3, and Mark 8:34 and decided that the words of Christ to the first disciples would also be their rule of life. A well-educated man, Peter was appointed the first minister-general of the Friars Minor in the fall of 1220, when Francis resigned his leadership. Peter died one year later, in 1221, at the Portiuncula, where he is also buried. Strangely, he does not appear as a character in any of the stories of *The Little Flowers*.

BROTHER GILES left the city of Assisi from the east gate that leads down to San Damiano one week after Bernard and Peter had joined St. Francis, seeking to join him, too. When Francis met Giles on the road, he led him to the chapel at Portiuncula and declared him the fourth brother (Francis was himself the first). One of the most legendary and important of the first friars, he traveled the world on early missions, sought martyrdom during the Crusades, and was with Francis when he died. After Francis's death, Giles was visited by popes, cardinals, and Bonaventure, and died an old man in 1262 in Assisi's neighboring town of Perugia, where Francis had assigned him and where Giles lived much of his life.

The primary author of The Little Flowers . . .

BROTHER UGOLINO BONISCAMBI lived a century after the first friars. He was likely born around 1260 in Monte Santa Maria, a municipality in the province of the Marches that is now called Montegiorgio. He died sometime around 1345. He is the primary compiler of the Latin work *Actus Beati Francisci et Sociorum Eius*, or "The Deeds of Blessed Francis and His Companions," from which the Italian *Fioretti di Santo Francesco d' Ascesi*, or "The Little Flowers of Saint Francis of Assisi," is a translation. We know very little about his life except that he spent his novitiate as a Franciscan in Roccabruna in the far northwest corner of Italy and was a friend of the angelic Pope Celestine V, who briefly ruled and then controversially resigned in 1294.

Some other important people mentioned in The Little Flowers . . .

BROTHER ANGELO TANCREDI was a knight before joining St. Francis, and his bearing always remained noble, despite voluntary poverty. He was the fortunate friar to accompany Francis on the walk that became the first sermon to the birds. He kept vigil at Clare's deathbed and testified at her canonization hearings. Angelo died in 1258 and is the third friar to be buried in the crypt of the Basilica. Some scholars have found evidence to suggest that Angelo and Francis may have been biological brothers.

BROTHER ANTHONY OF PADUA was born around 1195 and was a priest and monk of St. Augustine before joining the Franciscans in 1220. We know that Anthony was present at the General Chapter of 1221 when St. Francis presented the second edition of his *Rule*. He was known as a great thinker and theologian and was canonized by the same Pope Gregory IX who canonized Francis, and even more quickly (only one year after his death in 1231).

SISTER CLARE OF ASSISI called herself St. Francis's *pianticella*, or "little plant," who grew to show God's beauty and provide sustenance for the movement he started. By all accounts, she was a woman of great physical beauty and charm. The document known to history as Clare's *Acts*, written to support her canonization, mentions several marriage proposals. She left domestic life behind at the age of eighteen to become the first woman to follow Francis and was the founder of the Second Order of Franciscans, the Poor Clares. She was a woman of wisdom, sensitivity, and strength. She died on August 11, 1253.

BROTHER ELIAS was two years older than St. Francis and knew Francis from childhood. He became minister-general after Peter Catani in 1221, but his rule was controversial. He ruled until 1227, after which he oversaw the building of San Francesco in Assisi, and then once again he was elected minister-general in 1232. He was seen as despotic to some, even the essence of evil; this perspective comes through in *The Little Flowers* in a way that it doesn't always in earlier sources. Pope Gregory IX dismissed Elias from his position in 1239, and one year later, Elias joined Emperor Frederick II, a violent enemy of the Church, as an advisor. After a decade of serving Frederick II (whose mercenaries were famously repelled by St. Clare in an attempt to besiege San Damiano), Elias repented his sins to a priest and the excommunication placed on him was lifted. He died in 1253.

POPE GREGORY IX was Holy Father from 1227 to 1241. As Cardinal Ugolino, he was appointed by Pope Honorius III in 1217 to oversee St. Francis's enthusiastic young movement. He was elected pope just before Francis's death, oversaw his canonization, and brought great changes to his Order.

BROTHER JAMES OF MASSA was a legendary figure in the second generation of Franciscan Spirituals, respected by the prominent Brothers Giles and Juniper according to these stories. Born in the 1220s, he likely died in about 1305.

BROTHER JOHN OF LA VERNA lived from 1259 to 1322. He was born in Fermo in the Marches region, but spent most of his life associated with the mountain most revered in Italy for its associations with St. Francis. It was upon La Verna in the Tuscan Apennines in September 1224 that Francis received the stigmata. Brother John was one of the best friends of Jacopone of Todi, the famous Spiritual Franciscan poet.

BROTHER JOHN OF PARMA was minister-general of the Franciscan Order from 1247 to 1257, the one to serve in this capacity before Bonaventure's term. He resigned in

1257, unable to govern as a Spiritual in the midst of an Order increasingly dominated by Conventuals, and lived the life of a semihermit at Greccio, near Rieti, the place where St. Francis had enacted the first live nativity.

BROTHER JUNIPER was a close friend of St. Clare's, and was among those present at her death. He was a holy fool, and one of the strictest imitators of the life of Christ that the world has ever seen. St. Francis often praised him, believing that he probably possessed the greatest degree of self-knowledge of any of the brothers, and trusted him with various missions and responsibilities. He died in 1258.

BROTHER LEO was, with Angelo, the closest friend of St. Francis among the early friars. He was ordained a priest at some early point in the history of the movement, and seems to have become Francis's confessor, traveling with him all over Italy. Leo was present at the saint's death, and along with Angelo and Juniper, also at the death of St. Clare. He died an old man in 1271, and his burial place in the Basilica of St. Francis may be seen today in the crypt below the lower church.

BROTHER PETER OF MONTICELLO was a friar in the Marches. Born sometime before 1230, he was a leader among the second generation of Franciscans and among the Spirituals. He died in 1304.

BROTHER RUFINO was a cousin of St. Clare and called a saint by St. Francis. He joined Francis in 1210, one year after the first disciples. He was with Francis during the important early days in the caves of the Carceri when the friars were caring for lepers, and he was with Francis on La Verna when Francis received the stigmata. There are many stories of Rufino's having dark visions and temptations from the devil, with Francis counseling Rufino through these trials. Such stories might suggest that he was bipolar. Rufino lived to old age, longer than any of the other original twelve, dying in about 1280.

BROTHER SIMON was an early follower of St. Francis who died in about 1244 to 1245. He was one of the early Spirituals and probably among those who were banished to the Marches in the years after Francis's death.

FOR FURTHER READING

Other Excellent Editions of The Little Flowers
(plus selected secondary sources)

Each of these editions has been consulted in the creating of the present book.

Armstrong, Regis J. et al., eds. *Francis of Assisi: Early Documents.* Vol. 3. New York: New City Press, 2001.

Brown, Raphael, ed. *The Little Flowers of St. Francis: First Complete Edition.* New York: Image Books, 1958.

Doyle, Fr. Eric, OFM, STD, ed. *The Little Flowers of St. Francis, The Mirror of Perfection, and St. Bonaventure's Life of St. Francis.* Introduction by Fr. Hugh McKay. New York: Dutton, 1973.

Gardner, Edmund G. "The Little Flowers of St. Francis." In *St. Francis of Assisi 1226–1926: Essays in Commemoration,* 97–126. London: University of London Press, 1926.

Hopcke, Robert H., and Paul A. Schwartz. *Little Flowers of Francis of Assisi: A New Translation.* Boston: New Seeds, 2006.

Select Sources for Specific Stories

"ST. FRANCIS KEEPS LENT ON AN ISLAND IN PERUGIA" (AND OTHER STORIES ABOUT ST. FRANCIS'S PRAYER LIFE)

Bodo, Murray. *The Way of St. Francis: The Challenge of Franciscan Spirituality for Everyone.* Cincinnati: St. Anthony Messenger Press, 1995.

Sweeney, Jon M. *The St. Francis Prayer Book: A Guide to Deepen Your Spiritual Life.* Brewster, MA: Paraclete Press, 2004.

"ST. FRANCIS TAKES A SHIP TO SEE THE SULTAN"

Cusato, Michael F. "Francis of Assisi, the Crusades and Malek al-Kamil." In *The Early Franciscan Movement (1205–1239): History, Sources, and Hermeneutics,* 103–128. Spoleto, Italy: Fondazione Centro Italiano di Studi Sull'alto Medioevo, 2009.

Moses, Paul. *The Saint and the Sultan: The Crusades, Islam, and Francis of Assisi's Mission of Peace.* New York: Doubleday, 2009.

STORIES OF ST. ANTHONY OF PADUA

Cusato, Michael F. "Something's Lost and Must Be Found: The Recovery of the Historical Anthony of Padua." In *The Early Franciscan Movement (1205–1239): History, Sources, and Hermeneutics,* 317–37. Spoleto, Italy: Fondazione Centro Italiano di Studi Sull'alto Medioevo, 2009.

FOR MORE ABOUT ST. CLARE

Armstrong, Regis J., ed. *The Lady: Clare of Assisi—Early Documents.* New York: New City Press, 2006.

Sweeney, Jon M. *The St. Clare Prayer Book: Listening for God's Leading.* Brewster, MA: Paraclete Press, 2007.

Select Books on the Franciscan Spirituals

Burr, David. *The Spiritual Franciscans: From Protest to Persecution in the Century after Saint Francis.* University Park, PA: Pennsylvania State University Press, 2001.

Lambert, M.D. *Franciscan Poverty: The Doctrine of the Absolute Poverty of Christ and the Apostles in the Franciscan Order 1210–1323.* London: SPCK, 1961.

Select Biographies of St. Francis of Assisi

Armstrong, Regis J. et al., eds. *Francis of Assisi: Early Documents.* Vols. 1 and 2. New York: New City Press, 1999, 2000. (These contain all of the earliest biographies of the saint.)

Chesterton, G. K. *Saint Francis of Assisi.* Garden City, NY: Doubleday, 1957. (Originally published in 1924.)

Green, Julien. *God's Fool: The Life and Times of Francis of Assisi,* trans. Peter Heinegg. New York: HarperOne, 1987.

Habig, Marion A. *St. Francis of Assisi: Writings and Early Biographies— English Omnibus of the Sources for the Life of St. Francis.* 4th rev. ed. Chicago: Franciscan Herald Press, 1983. (This also contains all of the earliest biographies of the saint.)

Sabatier, Paul. *The Road to Assisi: The Essential Biography,* edited with introduction and annotations by Jon M. Sweeney. Brewster, MA: Paraclete Press, 2004. (Originally published in 1894.)

ACKNOWLEDGMENTS

Many thanks to the Franciscan scholar-saints of blessed memory who laid the foundation for our understanding of these tales today, including Luke Wadding, Paul Sabatier, G. K. Chesterton, Raphael Brown, John Moorman, and David Burr. And thanks, most of all, to Brothers Leo, Angelo, Rufino, Ugolino, and all the men and women who have lived in order to tell the story.

ABOUT PARACLETE PRESS

WHO WE ARE

Paraclete Press is a publisher of books, recordings, and DVDs on Christian spirituality. Our publishing represents a full expression of Christian belief and practice—from Catholic to Evangelical, from Protestant to Orthodox.

We are the publishing arm of the Community of Jesus, an ecumenical monastic community in the Benedictine tradition. As such, we are uniquely positioned in the marketplace without connection to a large corporation and with informal relationships to many branches and denominations of faith.

WHAT WE ARE DOING

PARACLETE PRESS BOOKS | Paraclete publishes books that show the richness and depth of what it means to be Christian. Although Benedictine spirituality is at the heart of all that we do, we publish books that reflect the Christian experience across many cultures, time periods, and houses of worship. We publish books that nourish the vibrant life of the church and its people.

We have several different series, including the best-selling Paraclete Essentials and Paraclete Giants series of classic texts in contemporary English; Voices from the Monastery—men and women monastics writing about living a spiritual life today; award-winning poetry; best-selling gift books for children on the occasions of baptism and first communion; and the Active Prayer Series that brings creativity and liveliness to any life of prayer.

MOUNT TABOR BOOKS | Paraclete's newest series, Mount Tabor Books, focuses on the arts and literature as well as liturgical worship and spirituality, and was created in conjunction with the Mount Tabor Ecumenical Centre for Art and Spirituality in Barga, Italy.

PARACLETE RECORDINGS | From Gregorian chant to contemporary American choral works, our recordings celebrate the best of sacred choral music composed through the centuries that create a space for heaven and earth to intersect. Paraclete Recordings is the record label representing the internationally acclaimed choir Gloriæ Dei Cantores, praised for their "rapt and fathomless spiritual intensity" by *American Record Guide*; the Gloriæ Dei Cantores Schola, specializing in the study and performance of Gregorian chant; and the other instrumental artists of the Arts Empowering Life Foundation.

Paraclete Press is also privileged to be the exclusive North American distributor of the recordings of the Monastic Choir of St. Peter's Abbey in Solesmes, France, long considered to be a leading authority on Gregorian chant.

PARACLETE VIDEO | Our DVDs offer spiritual help, healing, and biblical guidance for a broad range of life issues including grief and loss, marriage, forgiveness, facing death, bullying, addictions, Alzheimer's, and spiritual formation.

Learn more about us at our website:
www.paracletepress.com or phone us
toll-free at 1.800.451.5006

SCAN
TO
READ
MORE

Also Available from Paraclete Press...

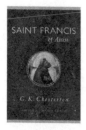

Saint Francis of Assisi
G. K. Chesterton

ISBN 978-1-61261-446-5
$10.99, Paperback

G. K. Chesterton seems to define "larger than life"—both in his own day, and in our own. Born in 1874, he penned novels, literary and social criticism, polemical essays, and spirituality in a style characterized by wit, humor, paradox, humility, and wonder. He has millions of devoted readers to this day, and many detractors, as well. It's tough to be neutral about so passionate a writer. Chesterton converted to Catholicism in 1922 and is best known for the mighty *Orthodoxy*, and the Father Brown detective stories.

The Complete Francis of Assisi:
His Life, the Complete Writings,
and *The Little Flowers*

ISBN 978-1-61261-688-9
$24.99, Paperback

There are many editions of the writings of St. Francis, and biographies about him, but here in one volume are both, plus the complete text of the late medieval work, *The Little Flowers*, which did more to establish the legend of the man than any other work. This "Paraclete Giants" edition includes the complete *Road to Assisi*, Paul Sabatier's groundbreaking and foundational biography of the saint, first published in French in 1894 and reissued and expanded in 2002; the complete *Francis in His Own Words: The Essential Writings*; and *The Little Flowers*, thus offering the best introduction to St. Francis yet available between two covers. Other Paraclete Giants include *The Complete Julian of Norwich* and *The Complete Introduction to the Devout Life*, both translated and introduced by Fr. John-Julian, OJN.

Available from most booksellers or through Paraclete Press:
www.paracletepress.com; 1-800-451-5006.